# Sometimes I don't like my kids!

# Sometimes I don't like my kids!

## Candace Schap

**Pacific Press Publishing Association**
Boise, Idaho
Oshawa, Ontario, Canada

Edited by Bonnie Widicker
Designed by Dennis Ferree
Cover by Steve Smallwood
Typeset in 11/13 Bookman


Copyright © 1991 by
Pacific Press Publishing Association
Printed in the United States of America
All Rights Reserved

**Library of Congress Cataloging-in-Publication Data**
Schap, Candace.
    Sometimes I don't like my kids / Candace Schap.
        p.   cm.
    Includes bibliographical references.
    ISBN 0-8163-1037-8
    1. Motherhood—Psychological aspects. 2. Motherhood—
Religious aspects—Christianity. I. Title.
    HQ759.S274      1991                    90-20963
    248.8'45—dc20                              CIP

91 92 93 94 95 • 5 4 3 2 1

# Dedication

To my husband, David, who patiently stepped over piles of laundry and dishes so I could write this; and to my kids who, in spite of it all, bring me great joy.

# Contents

# Preface

And I will give them one heart and one
way, that they may fear Me always, for their
own good, and for the good of their children
after them. And I will make an everlasting
covenant with them that I will not turn away
from them—to do them good; and I will put
the fear of Me in their hearts so that they
will not turn away from Me. And I will rejoice over them to do them good, and I will
faithfully plant them in this land with all My
heart and with all My soul (Jeremiah 32:39-
41, NASB).

These verses God gave me about the marriage
He had planned for me before I even knew my
husband. I have turned to them often to remind
myself that God's intentions toward me and my
family are for good.

The secret I have had to learn is the nature of
that "good." For a long time I interpreted His
"good" for us as meaning a prosperous and
happy life. I pictured myself as the mother
dressed in white eyelet, running hand in hand

with my family through a field of daisies.

Life has certainly not always—if ever—been like that. In fact, I have come to realize that the "good" He promised to do was to "plant me in the land," not to make life a bed of roses. I see "the land" as being His kingdom, which I entered when I first asked Him into my life.

He has been faithful to that covenant. He is even still in the process of making my family and me fit for His kingdom. He uses the rough times along the way to develop our characters.

I dedicate this book to Him, because I am confident of this very thing, that He who began a good work in me will perfect it until the day of Christ Jesus (see Philippians 1:6).

# Introduction

I sat on the sun porch, legs crossed, arms clasped tightly across my chest. To anyone alert to body language, mine was speaking volumes. I was fuming.

I had reason to be angry. With four hyper little children inside the house, I glared at the empty spot in the driveway where my husband's car should have been. How could David be so insensitive, on a day that had been about as rotten as they come? When I had called his office two hours earlier and his secretary said he was on his way home, I had been so touched. He was being sensitive to my needs, I thought, coming home early to give me a much-needed break.

But when he didn't pull into the driveway, I realized that he had gone to the golf course. It was something he did quite often, but I had just hoped today was different. After all, it had rained all morning; surely the course would be soggy. Would David really rather slosh through nine holes of so-so golf, I thought angrily, than do something nice for me?

I mentally ticked off the reasons that should

have brought him home. Any one of them alone should have earned me an afternoon off, but I had had them all piled on me at once. In addition to not feeling well, I also had two sick kids home from school. That meant four children ages six and under at home all day for two days straight. And because it was a rainy day, none of them could play outside.

Even now the thought of the living room made me shudder. An elaborate fort built out of couch and chair cushions stood right in front of the TV. How many times had I said, "Please don't take the cushions off the chairs" before I had finally given up? Then all the rainy-day projects lay scattered about. The girls had taken all my paper napkins and made clothes for their My Little Pony toys. They had brought out various size boxes to build My Little Pony penthouses.

And of course little Petey had contributed to the redecorating. He had tossed magazines about the room with gleeful abandon. When there were no more magazines to toss, he had started on the video and audio tapes.

Because I had not gotten my usual breaks from the kids that week, my stress level was higher than usual. The previous morning I had missed my Bible study. Our church supplies a sitter, and it is one of the few times during the week that I get to talk to grown-ups. Then today I had to cancel my weekly sitter, which meant no grocery shopping. I never had thought the day would come in which I would be upset at missing grocery shopping, but that day had arrived.

Way down deep I knew I should be praying about my anger, but I was afraid to take it to God. I knew His ways all too well. He would want me to give up my anger and, even worse, be nice to David. However, I also knew that resisting God on an issue never turns out well, so very reluctantly I breathed a small prayer for help in handling the situation.

I was interrupted by new sounds coming from the living room, but I just couldn't bring myself to check. Instead, I stared glumly at the empty driveway and plotted revenge. My prayer notwithstanding, the man did deserve at least a small smack on the wrist, didn't he? I came up with all sorts of tempting ideas, but finally settled on something I could realistically carry out. As soon as David set foot on the sun porch, the minute he walked in that door, I was going to get up, say, "See ya later," and take off. Let him deal with the craziness inside that house. What better way to teach him to appreciate me more?

But speaking of craziness, now what was that sound coming from the living room? It sounded like the fireplace screen being scraped across the hearth. If Petey got into the fireplace—I jumped to my feet.

Just then I spotted the familiar silver station wagon rounding the corner and heading up the street toward the house. Quickly I sat back down. A quick calculation had told me that the effect would be greater if I were sitting there scowling when he entered.

Then something almost mystical happened. As

he pulled into the driveway, David looked toward the porch, and our eyes met. In that brief moment, I saw things with such clarity that it almost frightened me. I saw in his face a look of surprise to see me sitting all alone on the porch. Instantly I realized that he was totally unaware of my state of mind over the events of the past few days. I felt my entire body relax. I knew I could still press the issue, still try to drive home the point that I needed him to be a little better tuned in to my ups and downs. But with a shrug of resignation, I made my choice: life is too short to spend in constant conflict with my best friend.

I'll bring it up later, I decided, after the children are in bed. I'll gently try to help him understand how much I need his support during times like these. But right now I have kids to feed and a living room to put back in order.

He came through the screen door with a look of sympathy on his face. "What's the matter?" he asked. "They getting to you in there?"

I sighed and stood to walk with him into the house. "Yeah, pretty much," I answered.

He put his arm around me in a gesture of comfort and understanding, and together we walked into the house to brave the chaos. He would never know how one little prayer had saved him from a miserable evening.

There was a time in my mothering experience when I would not have been capable of a response like that. I would have either slipped into a shell of depression or gone into a tirade, taking out my anger on anyone available.

After talking with many women, I have come to the conclusion that my experience is not unusual. I went through a particularly bad depression, more intense than some women may experience, but the principles and applications I learned while working through it would apply to any mother trying to get from one day to the next.

That is my first reason for deciding to write this book. I am not what is commonly called a "natural-born" mother. I went through a long period of time in which I had very negative feelings about my children and the whole experience of motherhood. During this time, I didn't dare to breathe a word about my attitude to my Christian friends. I was sure they would be shocked to hear such ugliness coming from an otherwise pretty nice Christian lady. I was sure their esteem for me would be instantly lowered, and that, coupled with my own low self-esteem, would crush whatever spirit I had left.

My fear of self-disclosure was based on experiences such as these:

One day I took a new friend out to my sun porch and showed her where I had set up my sewing machine for the summer. "This way I can do the sewing I love and still keep an eye on the kids in the yard," I explained. Then I added, "Do you like to sew?"

She smiled sweetly. "Oh, I don't do anything like that," she said. "I'd much rather play ball with my children."

Another friend, after listening to my tales of

woe about fresh-mouthed, active kids, said simply, "I can't identify with you. My kids just weren't allowed to act like that." And she was a mother of six!

Remarks like these can send me into a blue funk for days as I try to figure out where I've gone wrong or berate myself for my attitude. I don't have a natural desire to spend all my free time with my kids, and I admit my disciplining methods are not always consistent. In fact, there are days when I don't like one, some, or any of my children.

Now, of course, I know that many other mothers have similar feelings. Most of the friends I feared to share with secretly wished they had someone with whom they could be honest. Some of us were not born to be nurturers; we have to work at it. But we get the mistaken idea that we're the only mother in the world who sometimes has negative feelings about her kids. We need to hear other women say, "You feel like that sometimes too? I thought I was the only one!" Or, "You yell at your kids too? I was afraid I'd be thrown out of the church if anyone ever heard me!"

One day not too long ago, after I finally got the girls off to school, my husband observed, "Boy, you sure acted ugly this morning."

"What do you mean?" I asked, trying not to bristle.

"The kids were being good, and still you snapped at them."

The past three days had been bad, and I had

slipped into some old patterns in response. At one point I had even shouted at the four of them, "I'm sick of you all!"

Still hurting from the sting of my husband's reprimand but knowing it was time to get myself back on track, I sat down and stared at the wall in frustration. I began to berate myself, thinking, How can you think of writing a book like this when you behave so badly, when you're such a failure?

Of course, I'm not a failure. It was thoughts like these that prompted the second reason I decided to write. Though we never reach perfection in any area of our lives, for some reason we demand it of ourselves in mothering. I want to tell other mothers, You are not alone in your feelings of failure. You have lots of kindred spirits out here. The important thing is that you learn from your mistakes and do better the next time.

Which brings me to the third reason I wanted to share my experience. While it is certainly helpful to realize that we're not alone and that our negative feelings are natural, we cannot leave it there. We must learn to deal with these negative emotions. Moaning with your friends about how tough mothering is may be therapeutic for you, but it does nothing to help your children. And while this book is directed to mothers, the welfare of your children prompts me to write.

Negative emotions, allowed to remain and fester, will lead to some form of abuse, be it verbal or physical. That's why it is imperative that we deal with our anger and resentment promptly. During the worst of my depression, I found myself understanding how some women end up abusing their children. I could never condone it; I just understood how it could happen. And that scared me. Abuse had always been alien and repugnant to me, and I didn't want to understand it.

Motherhood is probably the single greatest learning experience and testing ground some of us will ever face. As in other aspects of life, it contains both good and bad. While it is true that the negative emotions are natural, they should not dominate. When they do, we know they are symptoms of something seriously wrong. We need to learn how to take control of the negatives—and even make them work for us.

As Christians, we can't do that without God. By trusting Him and opening our mother hearts to Him, we will not only grow as parents and women through the things we learn, we will also grow spiritually. On these pages I share with you how God took me through some negative, devastating times and brought me back to joy in Him and my family. My prayer is that it will help you in your own struggle.

Scripture praises a mother with these words: "Her children rise up and bless her; her husband also, and he praises her, saying: 'Many daughters have done nobly, but you excel them all' " (Proverbs 31:28, 29, NASB). With God's help, each one of us can be that woman!

# Chapter 1

## Birthing Is the Easy Part

"Stop pushing!" the nurse cried, and she shoved her hand between my legs to push the baby's head back in. Then she barked an order to her colleague to go get the doctor, turning back to me in time to repeat, "Don't push!"

Her command meant nothing to me, and I pushed with all the strength I could. Which wasn't much, considering I had been totally deadened in preparation for a caesarean section.

I had just spent thirteen hours in labor. Because my physician believed the cord was around the baby's neck, I was kept hooked to a monitor the entire eight hours I was at the hospital. The nurses insisted I lie in a certain position to help the baby get oxygen, but when I had trouble handling the contractions in that position, they threatened me with shots of Demeral. The oxygen mask strapped to my face left me disoriented, which made me cry, which made them threaten other medication. The following series of events—epidural; slower, weaker contractions; short respite from pain; return of pain; tears—led to the physician's order that I be prepared for a C-section.

My husband protested strongly that I had not been given a chance to birth this baby. As smugly as only a doctor can be when he has mere mortals in his complete control, my doctor declared, "I'll let her try pushing for a little while, but she's completely deadened and really won't be able to. This isn't going to work, and I can't give her very much time." Then he left. Even though dazed, I determined to push my baby out in order to prove him wrong to everyone present.

When the nurse said, "OK, now you can push," I concentrated every bit of my strength into pushing—the epidural notwithstanding.

At that moment she gave the aforementioned order to stop. I had worked thirteen torturous hours toward this precise moment, and she wanted me to stop? I pushed even harder against her restraining hand.

In moments the doctor was back, a look of shock crossing his face when he saw what I had accomplished in just those few minutes. I quickly filed that look of shock away, intending to do some gloating of my own when I reminisced on this day.

I saw my son emerge and crinkle his face in dismay. Little Peter Edward was finally here. Now we had the perfect family: two girls, aged six and four, and two boys, the other aged two. After cleaning him, weighing him, and getting his Apgar scores, a nurse brought him over to me.

"Here's your son, Mrs. Schap," the nurse said, beaming.

As I stared at that beautiful little creature, only one thought crossed my mind: get him away from me. "Give him to my husband," I said weakly.

She handed him to Daddy, who cooed enough for the two of us. I was tired, nauseated, and shaky, and I had absolutely no desire to hold him. I was sure they all thought I was some kind of monster, but even that couldn't move me. I asked for a basin to throw up in and sent Daddy and baby off to the nursery. I just wanted to be left alone.

If I had only known, I would have treasured more dearly my two days in the hospital. How could I know what bringing home baby number four was going to mean for my life? Indeed, being "left alone" was going to become such a rare situation that the desire for it would at times become an obsession.

When David and I were dating and it became obvious that our relationship was getting serious, I decided it was time to tell him my feelings on having children. I had no intention of having any—just in case that might affect our relationship.

I had given this careful thought for several years, and felt I had come up with three good reasons for my decision. (1) There was diabetes in my family, and I felt it would be unfair to pass that on to some poor little baby. (2) As a Christian, I couldn't stand the thought of subjecting an innocent child to the evil that was all around me. (3) I did not have a maternal bone in my body. While I thoroughly enjoyed being someone's beloved aunt, I had to know that I could hand the baby back to someone when the going got rough.

Any one of these reasons alone might not be sufficient, but I felt that the three of them combined compelled me to make the decision I had.

David heard me out and said he understood my feelings. He didn't dispute my reasoning or demand I change my mind. Neither did he tell me his dream of having a houseful of babies.

In truth, I never did change my mind. I just progressed, from a single woman who naturally had no place in her life for dependents, to a married woman who knew that our union would be immeasurably enriched by the addition of children.

As we saw it, we had the choice of becoming yuppies and filling our lives with possessions, or becoming parents and focusing our priorities on the family. I realize that being yuppies *and* parents at the same time is not mutually exclusive, but since we weren't yet either, we saw it as a clear choice between two lifestyles.

We chose family. We made a decision right at the beginning that we would never spend a lot of money on something unless it was for the family. Rather than Hawaiian getaways for David and me, we would get a camper that slept six. Rather than a ritzy house in the suburbs, we would find one that was stout and sturdy, with a good play yard instead of fine landscaping.

We made lots of other decisions, of course, pertaining to the raising of our little ones. We agreed on forms of discipline, on the importance of their spiritual and educational upbringing, on finances. In short, with all the confidence found only in the not-yet-parent, we felt that all we needed now was the baby—and we would be all set.

Our firstborn gave us no reason to feel we had been mistaken. Not only did we handle the practicalities of parenting well, we also seemed to be on a spiritual high. God seemed closer than ever with this little miracle of life in our midst. Even now, whenever I see a woman who has just had her first child, I feel a little twinge of envy. My first year with my first baby was a time of total joy.

I was a typical new mother. I was nervous on the one hand, sure if I didn't do things just right, I would ruin the rest of her life. On the other hand, I bragged about each new pound or smile as if they somehow reflected the great job I was doing.

When Elizabeth started to walk at nine months, I made the natural connection that someday she would be a brilliant neurosurgeon. More experienced mothers looked at me in pity as they saw my tiny girl rushing here and there, but I couldn't imagine anything I would rather do than chase her around. She brought out the best in me, and I liked who I was.

I couldn't wait to have another baby, to double our joy. Even though I'd had terrible morning sickness with Elizabeth and had had to spend two months in bed, I was willing to go through it again to make our family complete.

Just in case you're wondering why I relate average, common events and emotions, I have a purpose. I want you to see that I was a normal, average woman. I loved my babies and the whole process of birthing them. I was as ecstatic as any woman has ever been over the little creatures I had helped to create.

Another important aspect needs to be mentioned. I asked the Lord into my life when I was twelve years old. Our relationship had a slow and shaky start, but in my midtwenties it had become strong and solid. From that time on, I experienced the normal ups and downs of the Christian walk, but my commitment to faith and growth didn't significantly waver.

When I talk about some of the negative feelings I experienced later on, you should keep two things in mind: (1) I had a good life, with enough to eat, a decent home, and wonderful family and friends; I was not a person with mental or emotional problems; and I had a close relationship with God. (2) If I could experience these feelings, they could be found in anyone.

In rapid succession I presented the world with three more babies. None of the birthing experiences were smooth or easy. Like all new mothers, however, I enjoyed relating my birthing experiences to anyone who would listen. I thought of them fondly as my "war stories." "It's worth every minute of it when you hold that baby in your arms," we say dreamily.

We have been through hell and back. The pain is excruciating, we suffer one indignity after another as we are exposed to every intern and resident that happens through, and we totally lose control of our bodies. Birthing is one of the most stressful things a woman ever does in her life.

Ironically, mothers don't realize that birthing is the easy part. The hard stuff comes later.

# Chapter 2

## The Hard Stuff

What a joy it was bringing my new little boy home. I was aware, however, of a difference in my feelings this time—small things that had been a pleasure with the others now seemed more like work. Nursing was a chore. After six months I weaned him to a bottle, something I had sworn I'd never do. There was little time to spend nurturing him one-on-one.

In my birth announcements, I wrote about how overwhelmed we were with this wonderful gift from God. But deep inside I knew that, for me, making babies had lost its magic. The discovery was disappointing, but still it didn't seem to really make a difference in my life. I seemed to be infused with boundless energy—not only was my house clean, but I was even finding time to bake cookies.

You slip into the Supermom mode without even realizing it's happening. Not only was I working feverishly around the house, I was also trying to be the best mom on the block and working at the church in a number of capacities.

Whatever adrenalin was running me physically after the birth of Peter also had me emotionally convinced that I could do it all.

I suppose that's why it was so hard to handle when things began to come unglued. I just couldn't believe I was actually losing control. The public "me" and the real "me" were such different people that a great chasm seemed to open between the two. And I fell right into it.

A normal progression, confirmed by most women with whom I have spoken, occurs as you add each new child to the household. First babies are a time of wonder and inexpressible joy. You spend large parts of every day watching them stare cross-eyed at their hands and recording each smile and gurgle. Even difficult first babies do not fail to rouse parents to a fervor of love and fascination never before thought possible.

For me, whether to have the second baby didn't even need discussion. If one child had enriched our lives so much, imagine what two children would do! I blush to admit it, but my attitude went something like this: "I know how to do this now. Bringing number two home will be a cinch."

Precisely because such an attitude is widespread, bringing the second child home can be a terrible shock. You begin to suspect (and will learn for sure if you have a third child) that the effect of babies on a home can be measured on a scale similar to that of the Richter scale for earthquakes. Logically one might reason that two children means twice the work. It is a great blow to your confidence when you realize that, in actuality, each added child makes ten times more work than the previous one. The numbers rise exponentially, which means that the third child ends up causing one hundred times more work than the first, and the fourth brings it up to one thousand times more! Is it any wonder I was left reeling when the full effects of number four began to be felt?

You see, for six years I kept bringing home these cute, sweet little babies. Then one day I awoke and realized they had turned into children! They talked back, they made messes, and sometimes they said things like, "I hate you, Mommy."

When Peter was six months old, I found myself on a downward emotional spiral that would eventually deposit me into the worst depression I have ever experienced. Depression is never easy to handle, but the fact that I was a Christian made it doubly hard for me. I had been over a lot of testing ground in my walk with Christ, and now I felt I had reached a point of spiritual maturity that precluded allowing depression to overcome me.

God had taken me through every phase of my life, and I couldn't understand why He wasn't lifting me out of this or, worse, why I wasn't allowing Him to. He had taken me relatively unscathed through the dangerous teen years. When I rebelled and married a non-Christian man, He had been there to pick up the pieces when that man rejected me less than three years later. He took me through the single years, with times of great faith and growth tempered with times of wavering faith and loneliness. Then with remarriage, the start of my family, and involvement in a good church, I felt I had finally reached a point of trust and stability that would withstand an earthquake.

On the "Baby-Richter" scale, Peter was about an eight.

In the journal I kept during Elizabeth's first year, a typical entry went something like this: "I wanted to start this diary as a place to write my feelings, but it seems boring to just keep writing over and over how much I love you. Your presence overwhelms me. I can't believe how blessed we are to have you, and I have not been sorry for one second that we do."

A typical entry after Peter arrived said: "Just spent five minutes fighting with Becky because she doesn't like the bottle of bubble soap she's got. There are four bottles, and they are identical! Finally got them out of the house. Making dash for bathroom when Peter yells. Now I'm sitting here with these basics to do: dishes, kitchen needs floor washed and oven cleaned; living room, besides always every minute needing straightening, badly needs dusting and vacuuming; bedroom needs bed made, there are at least three loads of wash in the hamper, and dressers and closets are a mess; boys' room needs boxes of clothes put away; dining room needs dusting and vacuuming; big pile of mending; girls' room is a mess; den is a mess; bathroom is scuzzy; spare room has been slowly torn apart by kids; there are two loads of wash downstairs."

The difference in entries says it all. In one I thought only of the happiness my child had brought me; in the other I completely concentrated on the condition of my physical surroundings. My kids had stopped being a joy and wonder for me and were instead the cause of all my grief.

In the beginning it was just a feeling of helplessness. As the laundry piled up in the basement and the dust bunnies piled up in the rest of the house, I began to realize that there simply were not enough hours in the day to accomplish all I had to do. Beyond that, I did not have enough hands to do all the things that needed to be done simultaneously. It made me feel helpless, as though I could not handle the job I had taken on.

Slowly, over the weeks, that feeling of helplessness evolved into one of hopelessness. And it frightened me. I began to walk through the house in a near-stupor as I tried to shut out the noise and mess made by four lively children. I could barely command my head to rise off the pillow in the morning.

Most devastating was realizing how total and all-consuming the commitment to motherhood really was, and that I could not get out of it. The very fact that I could even consider wanting out scared the daylights out of me.

It seemed that the people in my life had drained me dry—my husband included. Rather than being my partner and ally, he became just another person making demands on my time and emotions. I truly believed I had very little left to give.

I felt totally exhausted, totally frustrated, totally trapped. After all, how do you turn your back on your children? There obviously was no escape. If this went on much longer, I didn't even know if I was going to be able to handle my most mundane daily chores.

My journal entries from those days are pathetic:

Tuesday: "Becky and Danny have me nuts today. They are either zombied-out in front of the TV, or they are fighting. Breakfast was 'dumb' and 'stupid.' Becky is the worst. She treats him terrible, taunting and teasing, yelling and hitting. I need to get away from this house and the kids once in a while. I need to have some time where there are no demands being made on me. Even when I go out for a while, there's the time pressure to be back to cook dinner or whatever. It would be heaven to get away for an overnighter, where there were no pressures. I could bathe and watch TV and call room service. I could read, write, make a phone call. I need a day like that."

Wednesday: "Yesterday got worse and worse. At one point I even swatted Petey for crying incessantly. Like that's going to stop him from crying! He was bereft and I wanted to die. I love him so dearly. David said I could go out that evening, but I knew I wouldn't. I can't *stand* shopping anymore. Today has been better, but I've gotten nothing accomplished. I'm too tired to do anything. I have to get it together."

Friday: "School is canceled because of ice. Do they know that means I'm stuck here with four kids? I am just not sure if I'm depressed or very tired. Right now the effect is the same—I don't function well. Yesterday I realized I had forgotten Becky's doctor appointment, and I burst into tears. That is not a sign of a woman who is handling things."

The feelings that enveloped my heart and soul over the next few months were so ugly I didn't even want to give them a close look. But I really didn't have much choice if I wanted to save my mental health.

Finally I made the decision to get professional help. I didn't have the money to go to the Christian counseling service, and I was just too embarrassed to admit to my pastor that I wasn't the competent figure I tried to portray. So instead I opted for my clinic's mental health service. I knew deep down that it wasn't the best direction to go, but I was desperate.

Though I was nervous about going, one aspect of the appointment appealed to me. Someone was actually going to sit down and let me talk about my problems for one whole hour. Without interrupting. I could let it all hang out because this person would never let any of my friends in on my secret life as a misfit.

The waiting room at the clinic was cold and colorless. For some reason the crowded waiting room surprised me. I looked at the faces around me, trying to feel some kinship with them. But I couldn't. Most of the people were unkempt and poorly dressed. I looked down at my stylish outfit and thought about the life I had. Very likely any one of the women sitting around me would have gladly swapped me even-up for whatever sadness had brought them here.

I began to feel uneasy. Counting my blessings was fairly easy. I was happily married. I had four beautiful children, all in good health. We had a good home, food on the table, cars that ran. We had just started attending a wonderful church and had many close Christian friends. I was afraid that my harried-housewife blues were going to sound petty compared to the stories some of these sad-looking people must have to tell.

The first question the psychiatrist asked me after receiving a quick rundown of my general symptoms was, "Have you seen your physician about this problem?" I meekly shook my head. It had never occurred to me that my depression could have physical origins. The thought only added to my uneasy feeling that I was wasting this man's time.

For the next forty-five minutes he asked me questions about my mother, my childhood, my husband's mother. He asked me if I was considering divorce. I was not feeling the anticipated release by talking through these things. Inside I was screaming, "You're psychoanalyzing me! All I want to know is how to handle these kids!"

That evening I told David about my visit with the therapist. I usually avoided discussion with him about my depression, because his lack of understanding only depressed me further. He could not grasp how it could be so bad that a little hard work and willpower couldn't pull me out of it. Up to this point, his answer to pulling me out of my funk was in getting organized and finding better ways to do my chores.

But that evening, as I described my terrible hopelessness, he seemed to be realizing its depth.

"I told a friend at work today that I was afraid my wife was having a nervous breakdown," he said.

Those words were the beginning of my healing. Trivial as they may seem, just knowing that he finally understood, that he wasn't going to give me any more housekeeping tips but was going to go deeper with me, helped give me just the strength I needed to begin the process of healing.

The next step, though obvious, had for some reason been out of my grasp. I had to let go and give it to God. As I thought about my disappointing visit with the therapist and how I had hoped that his advice would solve my problems, I came to a startling realization. I had the greatest power in the universe at my disposal, the Holy Spirit, and I had not even given Him a chance. I had cried to one or two friends, run to a psychiatrist, and then run myself crazy like the aimless dartings of a squirrel caught in traffic. And all along the power had been available.

Intellectually I knew and believed that God is involved in every detail of our lives. He wants us to come to Him with everything. But when I looked at myself honestly, I saw that I had been ashamed to admit even to God that I wasn't the supermom I had pretended to be.

Once I admitted my self-deception, I was able to ask for help. His help came—slowly. I wanted Him to make everything better overnight, but He knew there was a lot of work to do. My cry for help contained the implicit request that God change my outward circumstances so that life would be bearable. He could start with lifting the depression, and then I wouldn't mind if He straightened out my kids a little. But He did neither.

I began to sense that God was working on my attitude. Things around me definitely weren't changing—the laundry, clutter, and noise were all still there. But gradually my attitude toward these things began to change. I remember clearly the night I finally recognized that fact. I actually felt a great happiness that I could finally see the direction in which God was moving, and I knew that I wanted to allow Him to work in me, even if it was painful.

The time for total honesty had come. God had prepared my bruised psyche so I could now handle it. I had felt so guilty about how mean-spirited my feelings had become that I had actually tried to bury them, to deny they even existed. In *Women Under Stress,* Randy and Nanci Alcorn tell us that denying our emotions only compounds the stress, and that feeling guilty about them even helps to magnify the stress (p. 94). Clearly I had to take all the ugly emotions and expose them to the light. It was time to put names to them.

I found that three emotions were crippling me: resentment, anger, and disappointment. Naming them helped me to see something important—I had taken every negative aspect of my life as a mother and directed it outward. Not once had I looked to myself as a possible cause.

In *Managing Your Emotions,* Erwin Lutzer gives a description of depression that defined my condition perfectly. I recognize that depression is a complex condition that can result from numerous causes, but I have no doubt that mine had the spiritual causes described by Lutzer. "Prolonged depression comes when we allow our feelings to control us. Consequently, guilt is added to the disappointments we already have; soon we become negative, feel worthless, and we actually hate ourselves. Depression increases and there seems to be no way out" (page 46).

Then he continues with an insight I had not yet grasped. He says, "Such depression is a sign of spiritual failure. Sometimes we may be angry with God or filled with self-pity. We may not be willing to face these attitudes, but God is getting our attention; He is goading us into facing sins we have rationalized."

As I named the emotions and explored their

individual causes, I finally began to see that I was the source of the problem, and a remedy was readily available. It was not going to be found anywhere but in my relationship with God.

Each one of the emotions—resentment, anger, and disappointment—can destroy a person's self-esteem or relationships with others if left unchecked. The Alcorns say, "Nothing so poisons the mind and sours the soul as uncontrolled anger, resentment, and bitterness" (pp. 95, 96). Tim LaHaye, in *Spirit-Controlled Temperament,* says, "Grieving the Holy Spirit through anger, bitterness, wrath or other forms of human cussedness probably ruins more Christian testimonies than any other kind of sin" (p. 69). Lutzer adds that "it is uncontrolled anger that causes our problems. It ruptures relationships, it stifles spiritual growth, it gives place to the devil, . . . and it opens the door to sinning" (p. 94).

I came to realize how important it was that I understand these emotions and find what had activated them in my mothering experience.

*Anger:* Of course I was angry with my children. After all, they had been the ones who had turned my life upside down. But I was shocked at my inappropriate responses to that anger. I had reached points so low that it had taken every bit of self-restraint I could muster to avoid physically abusing my kids. I would hit walls, I would go into dark rooms and scream, and I would yell so loud at them that sometimes my throat would ache. I was desperately afraid that the day might come when I would lose that last shred of control.

It would also be fair to say I was angry with God. I had dedicated my children and myself to Him. I had chosen the noble profession of motherhood, giving up material luxuries to stay home with the children, and He had let it go sour.

*Resentment:* I was doing all the giving. Everyone else in my life seemed to be taking, taking, taking. Just once I wished one of them would act appreciative of my sacrificing. In my younger days I had been a very stylish, well-groomed woman. Now I was a drudge with limp, dull hair wearing sweat pants with holes in the knees. Wasn't this proof that I was nobly focusing on the needs of others rather than my own? Where were they for me? And when they could see I had drained myself dry, why did they just keep heaping more demands on me?

*Disappointment:* I was disappointed at how my life had turned out. I had nothing to call my own, nothing in life to give me pleasure. I had given up all my outside activities because I couldn't handle them and mothering too. So what did I have? My personal life was a mess, and the physical surroundings of my home matched perfectly. Every day when I had to survey this chaos, I would heave a sigh of disappointment and try to block it out of my mind.

Underlying these emotions was a terrible, pervading sense of hopelessness. I realized that there would be no point in finding ways to handle my emotions as long as the hopelessness remained. Somehow I had to get to the root of it, purge it once and for all. How, Lord? I cried. That was when He took me deep inside my suffering and forced me to face my sin.

# Chapter 3

## Dealing With the Hopelessness

The year was 1969. I had been out of high school for two years, living on my own in the big city. The man I had been dating for several months had just told me some shocking news. Not only was he married, he had three children and was still living with his family. He had decided to tell me the truth because an event that day caused him to fear I'd find out anyway; his wife had tried to shoot him. Could I ever forgive him?

I was nineteen years old, and he was the first and only man who had ever wanted to marry me. He was not a Christian, nor did he lead a "good" lifestyle. Did I love him? The answer to that is not even clear. One thing I did know—he said he loved me. I wasn't letting this one go.

I made my decision without taking time to think it over. "I already love you too much," I answered. "I have to forgive you."

I don't know if it was my birth order as a middle child or just some inborn weakness, but I had never in my life felt like I was "good enough." I was smart, but not "good enough" for straight A's. I looked OK, but not "good enough" to date the guys who appealed to me. I was nice, but not "good enough" to be with the "in" crowd. I had Christ's forgiveness, but was not "good enough" to have His fellowship or approval.

I had somehow gotten the idea that the answer to all my deficiencies was finding Mr. Right. In my fantasies, there was a man who was so in love with me that he would do anything to be with me. He would place me on the proverbial pedestal and be completely blind to my faults. I had always feared that most people, upon getting to know me, would decide they really didn't like me. But not this man. Whatever it was that would drive others away from me would not even be an issue for him. His love would be unconditional—all I had to do was love him in return. And we would all live happily ever after.

During the times when my disappointment in life and in God would get too hard to bear, I would hold that dream in front of me like a beacon of hope. When I finally did find a man who wanted to marry me, it simply did not matter that he already had a wife and children. I waited out his divorce and eloped with him before the ink was dry on the papers.

In the beginning we were happy, but things went quickly downhill. Within three years, it was over. The unspeakable had happened—even Mr. Right had rejected me. If only I were beautiful, I thought, he never would have left. Or, if only I were a good Christian, he would have been saved, and we would still be together. The same old fear still clung like a leech—I simply was not good enough to be loved.

As I struggled through my grief, I made a natural turn back to God. No matter how we live our lives, we usually keep our faith on standby for the times when we're hurting. What I found upon my return to God was so amazing that, to this day, I haven't gotten over the wonder of it. I did not have to look hard to find Him. He was still where I'd left Him all those years before. Not only was He still there, but rejoiced in my return. While He did allow me to reap the suffering I had sown with my sin, He still accepted me back unconditionally. He loved me.

For the first time I began to understand just what having God in my life really meant. He was constant. He was totally reliable—He would withdraw neither His love nor His Spirit. Nothing else around me could be described that way. No human beings, regardless of how much they love you, are completely dependable. People will never be able to live up to your needs and expectations. Not only can they not give you unconditional love, but they cannot be relied upon to give your life meaning and fulfillment. It can be snatched away too quickly.

As my relationship with God grew and matured over the years, I always remembered that first lesson. When eventually David and I married, I had no illusions. I loved this man, I would work to be happy with him, but in no way could he be the central meaning in my life.

I am not sure when or how it happened with my children. Probably when I brought the first one home. Infants are so untouched by the ugliness in life that one is tempted to place an almost spiritual aura about them.

Indeed, my first year with Elizabeth was perfection. She filled my heart with such joy I thought it would burst. I remember telling a friend, as we proudly walked our babies around the neighborhood in their strollers, that for the first time in my life, I was exactly where I wanted to be, doing exactly what I wanted to do.

Each birthing experience, although full of pain and hard work, had been precious and mystical. The act of creating had filled my life for six years. From the time I first became pregnant and had to deal with morning sickness, there was never a time until the last one was weaned that I wasn't pregnant, nursing, or in some other way baby-centered. Making babies was my reason for living for six long years.

But something had gone wrong. My reason for living had now started causing unmentionable emotions to well up in me—anger, disappointment, and hostility. Once I finally began to face my true feelings, I realized all too clearly how my kids had become the cause of my hopelessness; I thought my negative feelings for them couldn't be changed. Even though I had prayed my heart out that God would help me feel positive about mothering again, it hadn't worked. It seemed to be obvious that I had been right in my self-assessment—I did not have a maternal bone in my body. I decided that the best I could hope for was to somehow grit my teeth and get through the years until the children left for college. I would just have to rely on God to sustain me.

Then softly and quietly, God tapped me on the shoulder. "Are you trusting Me to sustain you?" He seemed to ask.

"Yes, Lord, of course. I always have."

"Are you trusting Me to fulfill your needs and give your life meaning?" He spoke to my heart.

"Yes, Lord. Of course I am. I always have."

"Then why are you so angry at your children because they're not doing it for you?"

"What?"

I had done it again. This time, instead of a man, I had focused my trust on my children. I had demanded that they fulfill my needs for self-worth and purpose. Upon their tiny shoulders I had placed the terrible burden of giving their mom meaning in her life.

The psalmist says, "Cast your burden upon the Lord, and He will sustain you" (Psalm 55:22, NASB). Not only does this verse indicate the Lord is strong enough to carry our burdens, but He then sustains us. He simultaneously carries the burden and guides us through the problem. As an adult, I am incapable of performing a feat like that. Yet I had asked my children to do that very thing for me.

Clearly I had some confessing and repenting to do—and I was happy to do so. I've been a Christian long enough to know that no real change can begin to take place until you've taken care of the sin. And unintentional as it had been, my misplaced trust and dependence was certainly sin. Its snowball effect had turned me into a rather unpleasant wife and mother.

I began to pray again for help with my mothering, this time with an expectant and almost excited air. For the first time in a long time, I felt like my prayers were effective and purposeful. Every morning I faced the world, sure that this would be the day in which I'd see the dramatic change in my circumstances that was going to make my life bearable again.

However, it didn't happen quite that way. Soon my prayers became more a question than a request: "Lord, You are doing something, aren't You?" Although the process of change had begun inside of me, I was now expecting it to shift to the things around me that negatively affected my existence. Second Corinthians 10:7 describes my viewpoint at that time. "You are looking at things as they are *outwardly*. If any one is confident in himself that he is Christ's, let him consider this again *within* himself" (NASB). Only slowly did it dawn on me that the process within had barely begun.

My relationship with God was now back on track, but now I needed to learn how to sustain it. I could only do that by changing my unbendable attitude about the way things "should be," and instead be realistic about the way they were.

Once I realized God's focus was on me and my

attitudes, I was eager to help Him get to work. My depression had been so oppressive that I was willing to do whatever it was going to take. If we had to start from square one again, so be it. Anything would be better than what I'd had.

While I was learning to deal with and improve the negatives in my life, things didn't happen in a neat succession of steps. But little by little, as I paid attention to the subtle working of God in my life—and also with the help of a lot of hindsight—I was able to see patterns of thought and action taking form. I've written them here for you in a methodical, step-by-step fashion in the hope that you can put these principles to work for yourself without having to go through the painful learning process that I did.

The first step to take in improving your attitude and performance as a mother is making sure your relationship with God is healthy. Check your focus: Does your hope for a happy life rest in God, or is it misplaced on your children, your mate, your job, or some other inappropriate object? Check your attitude: Are you willing to let God change you from within, or do you stubbornly cling to the belief that your troubles are the fault of those around you? Last, check your goals: Are you striving to honor God in whatever circumstances you have been placed, or are you clinging to old dreams or interests that conflict with your present responsibility?

The next step for me was to begin the process of changing my negative attitudes and emotions to something positive. God started that process by working on my resentment. He knew I would need all the people I had dismissed back on my side if I were going to have a total healing.

# Chapter 4

## Dealing With the Resentment

I resented everyone.

First, my family put unending demands on my time and fragile emotions. The old saying "Man's work ends at set of sun, but woman's work is never done" described my attitude exactly. My family wanted me to take care of their daily physical needs, starting with breakfast and ending with, well, the next breakfast. After all, I was on call all night long too. They wanted me to fill their emotional needs: comforting when needed, giving unconditional love at all times, and being romantic when my husband felt the urge. If I spent time on the house, I would get little hints that I was falling down in discipline or time spent with the children.  If I spent time with the kids, I would receive nudges about the housework. And from what I could gather from their actions, all they thought they owed me in return was a gift from the children on Mother's Day and an "I love you" once a day from Dad.

My church and friends made demands too. The church wanted me to teach children's

49

classes or serve on a board or sing in the choir. Each week at church I desperately tried to hold my little troop together for two hours, then would go home resenting having had to put on my "Suzy Christian" act. It was the same with my friends. There were only one or two to whom I would give any indication that all wasn't as it seemed. I could not bear to let them see that I wasn't the joyful Christian and all-sufficient mom I so desperately wanted to be. So I resented my friends because I had to keep up my act for them.

Of course, my neighborhood, my community—the whole world, it seemed—wanted something from me. They wanted me to make cookies for the school party, head the heart-fund drive on my block, go to zoning board meetings, march for causes—it never let up. I was a hornet's nest of resentment, getting more dangerous the more people poked at me.

It is easy to see that my perspective was warped. Obviously everyone in the world couldn't be wrong and I the only right one. After confessing all this lack of perception to the Lord—and I purposely stress that point—He gave me insight into the cause of my resentment and the way to deal with it.

Needless to say, the cause was *me*. That truth was a bitter pill to swallow, but the facts couldn't be denied. I had allowed my family to take advantage of me; I had refused to let my friends see the real me, warts and all; and I had not made use of the word *no* to my community. I knew God was right—I was going to have to accept responsibility for this particular pit into which I'd fallen. How could I change things now?

The solution came in one word: *honesty.*

The very simplicity of it caused me to heave a great sigh of thankfulness. I was experiencing the Bible promise, "The truth shall make you free" (John 8:32, NASB). I knew God wanted me to start speaking the truth. To be honest.

Being honest is scary. It's hard to admit you're not everything you've pretended to be. Since I was a mother of four, other mothers had looked to me as their resident expert. How did I admit to them I was as confused and frightened as they were? Younger Christian women had looked to me as a spiritual role model. How could I confess that, when put to the test, my faith had been weak and fragile? My family thought of me as the one person they could count on for love and support. How could I tell them I didn't like taking care of them anymore?

I started with my family, specifically my husband. He, more than anyone else, had been attuned to my misery of the past few months. He had been worried that I was on the verge of a breakdown, and I knew that he would want to know if there were tangible ways he could be of help. We talked for a long time and agreed on changes that could be made. I knew even as he agreed on certain points, however, that it would be up to me periodically to remind him if he slipped into old patterns. That would be difficult for me to put into practice, because up until then my method of reminding him about something was to pout for a few days until he noticed and asked what was wrong. I knew that pattern would have to change, that I would have to learn to be forthright. I also knew it would be a difficult adjustment for both of us.

And it was difficult. I remember at one point David lashing out at me. "I'm sick of hearing about all your needs!" he cried. "I've got pressures at work, and I don't need this too." But eventually we worked through all the bottled-up anger and resentments, and one day we realized we were functioning as a family again.

With the children it was not as easy. In their world, they are the center of the universe. It is very hard for them, especially the young ones, to even partially comprehend their mother's stress. I find that the best techniques in working with them are repetition and assignment.

*Repetition:* I sat the children down and explained how hard it is for mommy to do everything. After talking it over, they agreed that it really isn't fair for one person in the house to do all the work.

If you have a talk like this with your children, let me warn you that by tomorrow they will have forgotten the whole thing. That's where repetition comes in. I have a friend who says when her four-year-old gets too demanding or uncooperative, "I'm beginning to feel like Cinderella again." This brings Mommy's plight into an arena that the little girl can clearly grasp, and it usually spurs her to action. You can find your own ways to remind your children that families function best when all its members pitch in and help.

*Assignment:* While they may agree that Mom shouldn't get stuck with all the work, most kids are not going to volunteer for jobs. And when they do volunteer, they usually regret it when the actual work begins. Children need to know what duties are expected of them. Then when they balk, you don't need to yell or feel resentful. You simply say, "These are the rules we all agreed on, and you will do your job or face the loss of privileges." If you are firm and consistent, they will soon learn all their complaining won't get them out of doing the task.

When I tell my seven-year-old to set the table, sometimes her response is to stomp her feet, wrinkle her face, and wail, "I don't want to! I hate doing that! You're mean!" And once my five-year-old lamented, "I wish we could go back to the old way when you did everything." But now I can answer, "It's your job."

Next I had to learn to conquer the pride that affected my relationships outside of my family. Friends are amazing people. The minute I began to be honest that motherhood was making me a basket case, two things began to happen.

The first was that friends began to put themselves out for me. One brought us dinner one night. Another offered to take the kids for an afternoon. At first I felt guilty accepting these favors, because many of these women were mothers of one or two themselves. But then a close friend reprimanded me for those feelings. "I wouldn't offer if I didn't want you to take me up on it," she said firmly. "You're my friend and I want to help when I can. If I can't, I won't offer."

It had never occurred to me that we deprive our friends of a vital part of friendship when we don't allow them to help us. Galatians 6:2 tells us to "bear one another's burdens." When we're not honest, we hurt ourselves; people can't help when they don't know there's a need. But we also hurt them by depriving them of the chance to serve and be a friend.

The second thing that began to happen when I admitted my frustration was frequent expressions of thanks for my honesty. One woman said, "I always looked at you and felt inadequate. Here you had four kids and were doing great, and I am struggling so with my two. I know it sounds awful, but it's good to hear you're struggling too." Another said, "Thank you so much for what you said. I thought I was the only one in the world who was ugly to my kids."

Mothers are hurting because they think they are alone in their struggle. When we put up a false front, not only do we deprive ourselves of help and support, but we also deprive other women of the help and support they need.

The third step was to be honest with my church. I went to my pastor and very honestly told him that I could not handle any more responsibility at the moment. I chose the one position I thought I could do my best job in and then learned to say No to all other requests. It was hard at first. Many times Christians become experts at heaping guilt on themselves for saying No. After all, how can you refuse to teach the junior-high class if no one else has said Yes? It could be your fault they never hear about Christ. How can you say No to leading children's church when these people have done so much for your children already? In short, how can you say No to anything that is the Lord's work?

I had to learn to harden my heart to the most earnest requests. David and I were asked to sing with a small group for a special event at the church. "Just bring the kids to rehearsal," we were encouraged. "They'll be fine." Against our better judgment, we did just that. My husband spent almost the entire time chasing little ones off ladders and away from pianos. It was miserable. We had to take a firm stand after that. We now just say we cannot participate in anything that involves both of us. Maybe some people don't understand, but we know where our stress points are. We cannot please everyone anyway, so we have decided to put the health of our family relationship first.

Life was so much easier after that. Because I know there will be time in the future for me to collect for the heart fund and fight for causes, I can now say No without hesitation. And because I've gotten rid of so much of the excess responsibility I'd taken on, I now find I can happily say Yes to baking cookies for the kindergarten Christmas party.

Of course, I have not yet mentioned the most

important person we need to be honest with—
ourselves! In some way or another, we are all
trying to be Supermom and at the same time
denying it. We are not honest with ourselves
when we set our expectations so high they're
impossible to reach. Then we become angry with
ourselves for not performing. I used to think my
house must be a mess because I was lazy. It
didn't occur to me that anyone would have a
hard time keeping up with four perpetual whirl-
winds.

Sit down with yourself and let it all hang out.
So what if Mary Jo makes homemade bread
every week—I hate making homemade anything!
There, doesn't it feel better to admit it? So what
if Esther irons her sheets—I haven't ironed anything in six months! Each admission feels even
better than the last. My kids don't get a bath
every night, my curtains haven't been washed all
year, my oven still has Thanksgiving turkey
spills plastered on it—make your list as long as
you want.

Then decide which of these things you care
about changing and which you don't. If it makes
you miserable to have a dirty oven but not dusty
curtains, clean the oven and leave the curtains.

Hallelujah, we don't have to be Supermoms.
Each of us has her own strengths and weak-
nesses. The sooner we face up to our limitations,
the sooner we will learn to live within them. That
cannot help but relieve stress.

Last week at my Bible study group, a young
mother said, "I can't help it. When I look at other

women's houses and they're all so clean, I wonder what's wrong with me."

Laughingly I said, "OK, ladies, I'm having open house. Anytime one of you starts to feel like that, just come on over. You'll feel better right away!" My Supermom image has been blown. Gone are the wondering whispers of, "How does she do it?" But boy does it feel good to have realized that my definition of a "good" mom and reality are two different things. I have banished the "good" mom forever. Now I am me, backed by the Holy Spirit and some loving friends, doing the best I can for my family. While I'm always striving to do better, always willing to learn and grow, I'm doing it as me. Not Supermom, not "good" mom, just me.

# Chapter 5

## Dealing With the Anger

"Mom, can't you ever just listen to me?" my seven-year old cried.

I tried, but my anger just kept growing. "I don't want to listen to you," I practically yelled. "It's after ten o'clock at night, and I want some peace and quiet. I have a program I want to watch, but it's a grown-up program, and I can't watch it if you're here. Now go to bed." I turned my eyes from her, hoping if I concentrated hard enough on the newspaper in front of me, she would realize the conversation was finished.

But, instead, she worked herself up into one of her great dramatic performances. "You don't care about your family," she accused me through her tears. "All you care about is your favorite program."

Her words stung me, but I kept my tongue. Part of me was afraid she was right, and part of me was angry that she could make such an accusation to a woman who spent 90 percent of her time doing for her family.

"If you cared about your family, you wouldn't

59

be doing this to me!"

The anger began to pound in my chest again. I knew that it had built to a level far out of proportion to the situation, but I couldn't seem to get a grip on myself. I wanted to strike out at her, but, thankfully, angry as I was, I knew that would be wrong.

I stood there, torn between my anger with her and my desire to do the right thing for her. Because Elizabeth is such an actress, I had no idea whether her fear of going to bed alone was real or just some contrived manipulation to stay up later. Consequently, I had no idea what to do.

I tried to remember what the experts had said in all the parenting books and magazines I had read, but whatever I tried didn't seem to work. She was literally making me crazy. The thought occurred to me that I had better pray fast, but the truth is that I didn't want to give up my anger. Moms have rights, too, I thought heatedly. I have a right to some quiet time at night! I very reluctantly grumbled a prayer that went something like, "She's making me nuts. You better do something here, because I'm about to crack."

In frustration I turned off the TV. Was I supposed to let her sleep downstairs if she was too afraid to go upstairs? I turned out all the lights and let her get on the couch; then I went into the den and seethed.

This couldn't be right, I thought. I'm letting her rule the house.

I jumped up and stomped into the living room. "No, you're not going to do this to me," I said, pulling her by the hand. "You're going upstairs, and you're going to bed!" But what if she really was too frightened? Was I going to traumatize her for life? But if I let her stay downstairs, wouldn't that send her a signal that she could manipulate me?

When she was tucked into her bed, she was still sobbing. Through her tears she said plaintively, "Mom, you always tell me I should come and talk to you about things. But whenever I do, you just get mad and yell at me."

Another knife to the heart. This time, I knew she was right. I had been ranting and raving so hard, I hadn't even taken the time to talk with her rationally. I swallowed hard against my anger and the righteous indignation that tries to tell you the person deserves it, and I sat beside her on the bed. This time my silent prayer was repentant. To her I said gently, "I'm very sorry. What do you want to say to me?"

We talked for a while and did eventually come to a peaceful solution to that night's problem, but I went downstairs badly shaken. I had behaved terribly toward my daughter, and I didn't know what would have caused such behavior.

I knew better. I prayed again, and this time I was open to listening.

Part of my anger, I knew, stemmed from my desperate need for an hour or two of children-free time. I wanted to watch a grown-up program, so I had acted selfishly toward her in a bitter battle to protect my rights. We face this struggle all the time as parents, and it's one I fear will only get worse as they get older. Still, my extreme anger had been inappropriate.

I had been angry about losing my private time, but what had caused my anger to grow out of proportion? The answer I came upon was simple, and I almost felt stupid that I hadn't realized it before. I had been angry because I didn't know what to do. I wasn't angry with Elizabeth; I was angry at not knowing how to handle the situation. She had just been the poor unfortunate who took the brunt of that anger.

If I had known exactly what to do in the situation, I would have done it and gotten on with my evening. But I didn't. I was afraid, on the one hand, to traumatize Elizabeth by forcing her into her own room, afraid, on the other hand, to let her win some sort of power struggle with me. Either way, my ultimate goal was for a healthy, happy solution to the problem. My intentions were honorable. But not knowing how to achieve that goal, I let my frustration build into anger and my anger to sin.

I tried to remember other times when I had gotten irrationally angry with the children. A surprising number of times, the anger could be traced to this same root problem. When I didn't know how I was supposed to handle a situation, I got angry. Some people get nervous, some become wishy-washy or lenient, some withdraw into a shell. I become angry.

Pinpointing the cause of my anger was a great relief. It helped tremendously to know my anger didn't erupt because I was an evil-hearted mother, but because I so earnestly wanted to do the job well. It was not an uncontrollable character weakness, but an incorrect response to stressful situations that could be relearned. Also, by knowing the cause of my anger, I could submit it to God's lordship, asking Him to show me proper ways to deal with my frustration.

What we who struggle with anger need to do is address the problem at a time when we are not under pressure. Later, when the stress starts to build, we can turn to those strategies for anger control that we developed in our quiet times. Of course, the problem I've just discussed is only one source of the anger we face as mothers. But because I recognized and isolated the cause of my anger, I was able to face it as a single enemy instead of as an overwhelming horde of unidentified emotions.

I strongly recommend that you take some time to single out the various reasons for the anger you have faced in your mothering experience. I list a few of mine here to help you start your list, but we all face different stresses with different responses. Therefore, your list could be very different from mine.

1. The most obvious anger results from a child's misbehavior. This anger is natural and good if it motivates us to the discipline that is called for in the situation. Ephesians 4:26 says, "Be angry, and yet do not sin" (NASB). In other words, anger can be useful when directed at a situation that needs correcting. It becomes

wrong when we lash out with it. That is sin.

In my experience, I find this particular type of anger is rarely overwhelming if channeled properly. When I discipline promptly and thoughtfully, the anger is quickly replaced with the love of reconciliation. But when for some reason I let a situation drag on, or I simply respond to my children's behavior without thinking, then I usually end up sinning with my anger.

2. The second most frequent cause of anger I experience is feeling that my rights are threatened. This anger is not necessarily wrong if someone truly is taking advantage of us, but we need to handle the situation carefully.

I'm not yet completely comfortable in stating my needs. "I work hard for you guys all week, and now I need some appreciation/free time/space, etc." It never fails to make me feel terribly self-centered when I have to verbalize those needs. So, instead, I hold it inside until I'm ready to explode, and then in one moment of heat, I let them have it.

My husband and I noticed that our Sunday afternoons always seemed full of anger. When we finally took the time to analyze it, we were startled and embarrassed to admit that it was our fault—not the kids' fault. Sunday had always been our day to relax. My husband liked to go golfing or to lie back and watch a good video; while I liked to read, write, or do some other relaxing activity. Whenever a small voice would break my concentration, or play noise in the next room would make the video difficult to hear, our anger would mount. Unchecked, it was allowed to grow to proportions that caused us to lash out at our unsuspecting children.

3. I feel another anger when I know I haven't handled a situation correctly. In this case, I'm usually angry with myself, but when I don't handle this anger promptly, it can lead to sin in two ways.

The first is by redirecting that anger from myself to my children. As an example, consider the mother who, after spanking her child in anger, turns on him with the accusation, "Why do you get me so angry that I do things like that?" We don't like feeling guilty; but instead of confessing the first sin and having done with it, we try to remove the guilt by shifting the blame.

The second way that anger over handling a situation poorly leads to sin is when we allow guilt to fester. We walk around for days in a mood of recrimination: "How could I treat my beautiful child like that? I must be the worst mother in the world. When will I ever learn to respond in a Christlike way to such situations? God must be sick of me." Instead of claiming the promise in 1 John 1:9—which tells us God will promptly forgive and cleanse us from the sin we confess to Him—we punish ourselves by letting guilt rob us of joy.

4. A fourth anger I identified is anger purposely misdirected as manipulation. This scenario illustrates what I mean: My husband has done something to upset me. He has left the room without allowing me to vent my feelings on

the subject. Enter the toddler, whining for food. Instead of saying calmly, "No, it's too close to dinner," I say, "No, stop bothering me; you're driving me crazy." And I make sure to say it loud enough so the real object of my anger will hear it. I then proceed to treat everyone in that fashion until my husband either gets tired of it and makes amends or until he gets the point and comes to talk about it.

When we isolate various types of anger instead of looking at them as one giant emotion, they lose some of their power to overwhelm us. We can then begin to relearn our responses to anger. We can use specific ways to deal with each case, but two principles apply to all cases.

Most important, we need to submit our anger to God. Confess your anger, being specific about the times you know you're at your worst. Accept forgiveness for it. Then ask God to help you discover ways to handle the anger.

The second step is more difficult, but practice makes it easier. The minute we realize the anger is building, we need to call a "timeout." Immediately try to identify the real source of your anger and give it a name. Then recall the ways you listed earlier to deal with this particular kind of anger. Say a quick prayer, and get on with whatever you have to do.

The specific suggestions listed below are only to get you started on making your own list of coping techniques.

1. One way to control your anger when your

children misbehave is to deal with it immediately. When I delay and simply issue a series of threats from the next room, I usually end up exploding. But when I deal with the behavior when it first occurs, I usually avoid the explosion that follows a buildup of frustration. I also then portray to the children a parent who is in control—and that, in itself, commands more respect.

Another way to avoid reacting with anger when your children misbehave is matching—ahead of time—appropriate disciplines with various behaviors. Many of us randomly choose when the crisis arises, and have never really given any thought to how we want to discipline. You should decide in advance what offenses deserve a spanking so you don't smack willy-nilly every time the children look cross-eyed at each other. What will you do for biting or name-calling or backtalking? Decide this beforehand and be consistent in your discipline. When you feel in control, you are less likely to react with inappropriate anger.

2. You can do several practical things when you feel unappreciated, overworked, or overlooked by your family. If you feel that your husband doesn't give you enough free time away from home, you need to tell him so. Many times husbands don't realize that being homebound is a problem. Then between the two of you, agree on a more equitable arrangement. For some it may be a regular day off. For others, an agreement to set aside money for a baby sitter to be

used at Mom's discretion. Whatever the plan, it is vital that together you reach an agreement. Being able to calmly and rationally fall back on your agreement will defuse many arguments.

Your husband needs to be the one who reminds the kids to appreciate Mom. He needs to be gently pointing out to them the way Mom works for them all day and to intervene when their demands get too selfish and strident. Mom should not have to remind the children how much they should appreciate her. This only leads to resentment on everyone's part.

3. When we don't know what to do, we usually get frustrated and angry. It only makes sense, then, that if we are prepared, we will not react with anger. I call this being an educated mom. Read books on discipline, bed-wetting, potty-training, etc. Read parenting magazines, especially the Christian ones, that are packed full of helps for the harried mother. Arm yourself with knowledge—prepare for the problem before it comes up.

This doesn't mean you'll know how to handle everything, of course. But that's where the "timeout" comes into play. Though it often seems like it, most situations don't have to be taken care of within the following thirty seconds. Have your child sit in a "timeout" chair of his or her own while you take some action. Call a friend for quick advice, run get the book you remember had mentioned this problem, or simply decide if this is an issue you can put off until later when you've had a chance to get your answers. In any case, the timeout serves to defuse your anger so you can be in control of what happens next.

4. When we are angry at someone else and take it out on our kids, they pass the anger right along. When I yell at my five-year-old without cause, she quite often leaves the room and vents her anger on the three-year-old. In such a cycle, everyone in the family is learning negative behavior patterns.

Part of the problem can usually be traced to communication problems between you and your spouse. You need to learn new ways of handling your anger with each other. Excellent books showing couples how to improve their communication are on the market. Read them! And after you've read books on communication, discuss them with your spouse. You have to agree that certain behaviors are improper, especially when they hurt the children. Just agreeing, of course, won't stop the arguments. But when you work together on the problem, it makes you both more aware of what is happening. The more often you respond correctly, the more quickly will the new response become part of your behavior.

And no matter what caused the anger, use your prayer and "timeout"! Lashing out in anger at any time is inappropriate. If you find yourself responding without control, stop and pray—no matter how little you may want to.

Proverbs 16:32 says, "He who is slow to anger is better than the mighty," and Proverbs 17:27 tells us, "He who has a cool spirit is a man of understanding" (NASB). Only when you have your anger under control can you deal with the problem at hand in a way that honors God and your family.

# Chapter 6

## Dealing With the Disappointment

One sunny morning, bright and early, I dressed in my best idea of what a hiker should wear and then packed sandwiches and apples for three into a little pink backpack.

This was the day I was going to reclaim one of the great loves of my life—communing with nature! The idea turned out to be a lot loftier than the reality. In my single days and on into the early years of marriage, I had loved hiking and being outdoors. It had become a tonic of sorts, something I treated myself to when big-city life distorted my perspective. I considered the quiet and freshness of walking in the woods or relaxing at a campsite to be indispensable pleasures.

I know it was naive, but it never occurred to me that the demands of mothering would crowd time in nature out of my life. When I had my first baby, I was full of the normal resolutions of the new mother: I was going to handle things better than those who had gone before me. I figured that, whatever it was I wanted to do, I would simply pack up baby and make her part of the activity. I tried it with one, and even had some minor success with two. But three proved my undoing.

So I wasn't all that surprised when I recognized one of my negative emotions as disappointment. I was very disappointed at how many activities I had had to give up. I ticked them off in my mind one by one: hiking, camping, reading, sewing, golfing, needlework, and decorating my treasured dollhouse. I gave up some activities because I lacked time or energy; I gave up others because of the hassles involved in hiring a baby sitter, wasting half my time keeping little hands out of my equipment, or feeling exasperated because projects took forever to complete. I envied the women who seemed to be able to incorporate their children into their interests or who had the ability to work around them. However, I found it almost impossible to do those things without ending up frustrated and wishing I hadn't bothered trying. Consequently, I put them all away. I no longer had anything that was just mine, no outlet for either frustration or creativity.

Now, however, with my renewed vigor and outlook, I was ready to pick up my acquaintance with some of those old friends. I had decided that hiking would be a good place to start. It would get me out of the house, I could involve the girls (Dad would be stuck with only two kids for the day), and it was inexpensive. A scouting friend had recommended a location, and now we had reached the big day.

We parked the car at the office of the Audubon

wildlife preserve and went inside to pay the entrance fee. Then we walked over to a little pond and stopped to eat our sandwiches. From there it was a very short walk to the trailhead. Before we could reach it, however, I heard four-year-old Becky whimper, "Can we go home now? I'm tired of hiking."

My balloon punctured, I had to give myself a good talking to. I would not revert to my old pattern of angry words and sullen pouting if the kids did not respond to this effort the way I had hoped. I was going to go with the flow, changing plans as needed to keep the outing happy.

Accidentally, I learned a valuable tip for hiking with small children. Stick to short trails that have very specific goals to aim for. Our first goal was a huge sugar maple that the girls went wild climbing while I tried to capture their interest in the fact that it was 200 years old and the biggest of its kind in the United States. Then we headed for a glacier boulder. They crawled into the little niches formed by broken pieces at the base and ate their apples, while I explained about the huge ocean of ice that had brought the boulder there. My third goal had been to reach the top of the hill, but, noting their flagging energy, I stifled my desire to see the fantastic view promised in the guidebook. Instead, we headed for another pond, which turned out to be inhabited by goldfish and giant green bullfrogs. We counted frogs until I noticed Becky doing a strange dance, and we had to rush to find the nearest bathroom.

Altogether we had walked about a half mile,

only a fraction of what I would have done on my own. But it had been a wonderful day. We had learned a little and had enjoyed each other's company. Best of all, the girls had been totally enthralled with the pleasures of nature.

My reward came when Elizabeth hugged me and said, "Thanks for taking us hiking, Mom. It was great." We climbed into the car and began a very quiet drive home as the girls started dozing off. Suddenly Becky's voice broke the silence.

"Mom?"

"Yes, Honey?" In the rearview mirror I could see her pull her blankie away from her sleepy face so she could speak.

"Don't ever take me hiking again, OK?"

However, just two weeks later, Becky asked me to take her hiking for her birthday. This time we made it to the top of the hill.

It should be obvious that you can't continue everything you once did in your spare time. For one thing, you'll have almost no spare time. Often you'll have less money for hobbies and recreation; your energy will go for homemaking and mothering. Instead of the long list of pleasures I once had enjoyed, I had to content myself with two or three activities.

As you start to revamp your list, you will have to keep in mind both the style of your family and also how much you are willing to compromise. Some items will not have to be dropped from the list but, like my hiking, can be adapted to fit your schedule and family needs. For example, I love to read, and a 300-page book used to take me two days to finish. As my time became limited, it was taking me weeks to finish a book. Because I just wasn't enjoying it anymore, I quit trying to read altogether. When revamping my list, I realized that I had already stumbled onto a simple solution. I realized that magazines, with their short articles and decreased demand for complete concentration, could fill my desire for reading. I now subscribe to several magazines on a variety of topics—everything from *Backpacker* to *Writer's Digest* to *Good Housekeeping*—and am able to keep reading on my list without disrupting my responsibilities to my family and home.

I approached each item on my list this way. I simply cannot abide sewing a garment if it takes more than one or two sittings at the machine to complete—in other words, this is a compromise I am not willing to make—so I decided that sewing is something I will come back to when all four children are in school. Golfing, which I quit when I became pregnant, is expensive and demands a large time commitment, so I will put it on my list of things to look forward to in retirement. While I cannot afford the time to always have a needlework project going, I can still plan to do one or two items a year as gifts, thus justifying the time and expense. The dollhouse can wait until there are no chubby little fingers itching to take it apart again.

Because I went through the list myself and—after weighing the pros and cons—chose items I would remove, I did not resent the outcome. My husband cooperates in giving me sufficient time for myself and also in seeing that my need for satisfying outlets is respected.

The second major area that caused me to become disappointed with my life was the condition of my surroundings. The house had become such a mess that it alone could have caused a major setback in the healing I was experiencing. I knew I had to figure out some way, short of hiring a maid, to keep the mess to a minimum and still not demand more of myself than I could deliver.

The biggest obstacle was the enormity of the job. Every morning when I awoke, I would look at all nine rooms that needed cleaning, and I would become nearly immobilized by the overwhelming job. Because I knew I couldn't do it all, quite often I did nothing. I didn't even know where to start. So if the size of the job was the problem, it made sense that I needed to break it into smaller, more manageable parts.

The best way for an unorganized person like me to start getting something done is to make a schedule. I hate schedules, but I found one that worked for me. I've tried many types of schedules. Once, after becoming frustrated with myself for not accomplishing anything during the day, I made myself an hour-by-hour schedule. At 10:00 a.m. I would be doing laundry; at 7:15 p.m. I would be reading a bedtime story. Needless to say, that schedule didn't work. I discovered that for the unorganized person, the key word is *simplify*.

So I took out my calendar and began to assign each room to a specific day of the week. The schedule went like this:

Monday: living room, dining room
Tuesday: den, porch
Wednesday: kitchen
Thursday: master bedroom, bath
Friday: boys' room, girls' room

Your preliminary schedule is not written in stone. As you experiment with the workload of each room, you may wish to pair them differently. The den and the porch are both light-work rooms for me, so I put them together on my grocery shopping day. The kitchen gets its own day because I usually end up working on it all day long.

I laid two ground rules for myself. (1) Once a room had been thoroughly cleaned for the week, I would allow myself to ignore it the rest of the week except for some minor straightening. (2) If for some reason a room could not be cleaned on its day, I would not put pressure on myself. I could wait.

The basic structure of my plan took a lot of weight off my shoulders. I had the wonderful freedom of knowing that each room would eventually get cleaned that week. I did not have to become upset by the kitchen floor getting messy—it would definitely get washed on Wednesday. In fact, under this system my floor was getting washed much more often than it had when I had tried to clean the entire house every single day.

As I worked on my system a little more, I found it helpful to make an actual list of chores for each room. I listed the chores in order of their priority, so that the major cleaning would always be sure to get done. Minor chores could be put off, if need be. For example, under "living room" I had listed:

1. Straighten. (Each item that doesn't belong in the living room must be put in its place.)
2. Dust thoroughly.
3. Vacuum, also using the edge attachment.
4. Clean the mantle. (Our mantle collects everything that the family can't find another place for.)
5. Clean windows and TV screen.
6. Sweep ceiling for cobwebs.

Sweeping ceilings for cobwebs had not been a regular part of my cleaning routine before. But now, because I wasn't also trying to clean seven other rooms that same day, I had the luxury of time to do it.

I think my kitchen was one of the major beneficiaries of the new system. In my house, the kitchen counters are the place where mail, bills, school papers, things I need to remember to do are routinely deposited. Those piles of clutter are now on the list of chores. The list looks something like this:

1. Clean piles of clutter. (Merely shuffling the papers around is not allowed. I have to handle each item before I move on to the

next. Bills either get filed or paid. School papers get tossed or put away, etc. This is one of the reasons the kitchen gets a day all to itself.)

2. Wash floor.
3. Wash cabinets and baseboards. (This cleaning usually had happened only when out-of-town visitors were coming!)
4. Scrub sink.
5. Clean refrigerator.

I'm thinking about adding menu planning to that list, which illustrates the beauty of this system. I can switch the kitchen to Tuesday, move grocery shopping to Wednesday, and then be able to plan menus the day before I shop. This may all sound rather basic to you, but that's exactly why it works. It is simple.

At this stage I began to realize that it would be important for me to set some priorities in running my household. I often hear mothers say, "I didn't get anything done today. The baby kept wanting me to hold her or play with her." I remember the first time I made that remark to my husband. He answered kindly, "Then you did get something done today—the most important thing you have to do. You loved your baby."

When it comes right down to it, what is more important? That the dishes are done, or that your child learns about love and caring from a parent who has time for him or her? I'm not talking about writing your child into the schedule. Your schedule should be flexible enough that you aren't put into a frenzy if Johnny needs extra help with his homework or if Sandra is teething and needs lots of holding. Make sure your children get your quality time, not your left-over time.

The people in your house are, after all, the reason for everything else you do. Nurturing, caring, loving—all should come before anything else. If you can spend fifteen minutes rolling around on the rug with your toddler, let the dishes sit for that fifteen minutes. If you're rolling around on a vacuumed rug, you are already way ahead of the game anyway.

Ask yourself these questions: What things have to be done to keep your self-esteem from plummeting? To keep the family functioning? Do you care if your bed is made? If yes, make it! Don't let its rumpled condition ruin your day. If not, close your bedroom door without guilt. Obviously the bathroom needs to be scrubbed every week, but does the oven? And another important question: Is my house tidy enough that I won't be embarrassed if the meter reader knocks on the door?

My system soon evolved into a daily pattern for me. It was comforting, because it made the day something I didn't have to fret over. The trick is getting started. On mornings when all I want to do is begin the newspaper crossword puzzle or turn on a morning talkshow, I stop myself. The important thing is not to sit down. Once I'm down, it's much harder to get up and get going. Get to work immediately. When you look at a chore, it's OK to think, "I don't want to do that," but then you've got to do it anyway.

I start my day by making the bed and quickly straightening the rooms I spend most of my time in. Then the rest of the morning I concentrate on the room of the day. At noon, I feed the kids, put Peter down for his nap, and take my "break."

The break is very important and shouldn't be neglected. I used to feel guilty about taking the time, but then I remembered my days as a working woman. It was mandated by law that employees be given a certain amount of time every day for lunch and breaks. Why should it be any different for the homemaker who is on duty twenty-four hours a day—not just nine-to-five? If you don't take care of yourself, there will be no one to take care of the rest of the family. You need to schedule some time for yourself in the middle of the day, so you can rest and recharge for the busy afternoon ahead when the children get home from school and dinner preparations have to start. You won't get another break until they are all in bed asleep.

I take an hour and a half for lunch. My only rule is that the time be reserved for leisure—for me. No ironing while I watch TV, no balancing the checkbook while I eat. That time is reserved for reading, writing letters, or just lying there doing nothing. It was hard to learn how to relax without guilt, but now I look forward eagerly to that time of day as my reward for working hard all morning. (Which gives me incentive to actually work hard—otherwise I would definitely feel guilty taking the time!)

After lunch I try to fit in some of the other chores that aren't on the room schedule. Laundry, bookkeeping, ironing, mending, menu-planning all come under this category. As I suggested before, grocery shopping should be scheduled to fall on the day of your easiest rooms to clean. If you go to a Bible study, bowl, or do some other activity one day a week, you will have to make a special effort not to neglect what needs doing the rest of the day.

I'll slip in a helpful hint here that has proven useful to me. Wherever possible, combine chores. Do two things at one time. For me, this means when I go upstairs to make the beds, I also grab a pile of the things that have been accumulating on the stairs. I put them away quickly, then make the beds. Another example: When the baby is old enough to play in the tub without Mom hovering, but not old enough to be left alone, put that time to work. I clean the sink and the mirror or prepare for the children's class I teach at church. I'm still there to smile and encourage the little one, but when bathtime is over, I have also gotten a couple of little chores out of the way. When a friend who likes to stay on the phone and chat calls me, I do dishes or start dinner preparations while we talk. Not only am I getting something done, but the job is much more pleasant.

I realize that a lot of what I have been saying here is directed more to the stay-at-home mom. But this same principle can be put to work by the working mother. A simple schedule that spreads the work out over a week (or even two weeks, if necessary) will relieve the stress of feeling like you have to "clean house" every night.

I had to learn how to organize my thoughts as well as my schedule. I bought a notebook and placed it by my telephone. Each day I would start a new page. Every time I remembered something I had to do or someone I had to call, I wrote it on that page. Everything gets written down—calling the doctor, baking cookies for the school party, or lining up a soloist for the women's group meeting. When something got done, it got crossed off. Anything that isn't crossed off at the end of the day gets moved to the top of the next page, with new things being added at the bottom. (If you keep your list in a smaller notebook, you can also carry it with you.)

This system takes discipline in getting started. At first I could never remember to enter things in the notebook. Then once I had entered something, I would forget to check the notebook for what I had to do. But with a little perseverance, the system soon became second nature. You will be surprised how difficult it will become for you to live without your notebook. And you will delight at how much more efficient you become.

Two negative factors that seem to be inherent to motherhood are stress and guilt. Whenever we discover methods or tools that will relieve either one or both, it is worth giving them a try. To be the best we can be for our families, and still take care of our own needs, we must face these two enemies head on. It will take a little work to develop these skills, but once we have, they will become our best friends.

Truthfully, I would much rather have to conform, however reluctantly, to a schedule than to put up with any more stress or guilt than necessary.

# Chapter 7

## Tools for Problem Solving

Throughout my time of exploration and discovery, I had noticed two distinct patterns evolving in my efforts at problem solving. When I realized that I had used these principles again and again by accident, it occurred to me that I should name and describe these tools. That way I could purposefully apply them to a situation.

I share them with you here.

*Relearning.* I'm not sure this is so much a tool as it is an attitude. But it's necessary if we want to successfully change our negative patterns.

Even though millions of women have been mothers before me, motherhood is totally new for me. In fact, every minute of it is new. You never have it figured out. Just when you think you do, the kids have entered a new phase, or you've added one more, and everything changes.

"Relearning" is what I call the flexible attitude that says, "OK, maybe what I've done before won't work here. Maybe I need to be willing to come up with something new." This attitude can play a big part in even the mundane things of life. I had been living on my own and cleaning my own house for fourteen years before I started having children. As far as I was concerned, I knew how to clean a house. Granted, my way to clean a house was generally not to bother. (I remember with great embarrassment the time a policeman came in to investigate after my apartment had been broken into. He was dismayed at how the thief had ransacked my bedroom. I was even more dismayed to have to admit that it simply looked normal.) Obviously, that method doesn't work well when six people have to live in the same house and four of them are under the age of six. Finally I had to admit, "Maybe my way isn't working," and only then did I become flexible enough to find a method that fit my new situation.

By the time I had my fourth baby, I was under the false impression that I should surely know the ropes by now. I would feel ashamed of myself when a situation would come up that I couldn't handle. I remember all too well the day I took three of the children shopping with me. By the time we left the store, I was such a wreck that I stood in the parking lot and cried. Occurrences like that did not do much to make me feel like the capable adult I had once been. I had once managed an office; now I couldn't even manage three little children.

I had not realized how inflexible I was. Pride kept me from admitting that when it came to raising children, I need uneducation. Nothing I had learned up until then was applicable. It was time to go back to school and learn techniques on handling children.

This fact was vividly brought home to me when we took our very first family vacation. It just never occurred to me that vacationing with the family would have to be done differently from the vacations I had taken before. You plan how you'll travel, where you'll stay, and how you'll pay for it, right?

The trip we were making was a ten-day excursion to Grandma's house in Florida. We did at least have the presence of mind to know that flying with four small children would need some careful planning. What would we take on the plane with us? How would we handle in-flight meals? Who would sit where? Other than that, we pretty much organized our actual stay in Florida as we had any other trip we had taken in the early years of our marriage.

We converged on Grandma's house like an invading horde. By the time we left, I was depressed and exhausted, David and I were still trying to patch things up from one argument too many, and even Grandma was getting short-tempered.

Back at home, I walked around for days feeling depressed and defeated. What on earth was wrong with me? Here I was, a mother of four children, and I still couldn't handle even something so simple as a vacation. One day the light finally dawned. (It couldn't have been the result of all that desperate praying, could it?) I had taken a vacation with four kids and had done it with one-kid expectations.

That may seem like a simple enough revelation, but for me it was earthshaking. I suddenly realized that what I needed was to relearn how to take a vacation! The best part was realizing there was nothing wrong with my ignorance—birthing four babies did not make me an automatic expert on the ins and outs of handling them.

The simple concept so excited me that I tried to find other areas where it had been or could be applicable. I found so many practical skills that I needed to relearn. For example, cooking meals. If the five-o'clock rush was too stressful, could I prepare part of the meal earlier in the day? When I stopped and thought about it, I had already relearned housekeeping techniques, shopping-day strategies, and how to pursue my personal interests. I could probably apply this principle to a lot more things.

I realized that I was also in the process of relearning attitudes. For example, I was letting go of the concept that my kids and their possessions were intruders, cluttering up my house and life. Instead I was learning to think of them as real people. Rather than trying to adapt myself, I had been trying to mold my little ones into the niche I had carved out for them, forcing them to conform to my expectations.

It was liberating to realize that so many difficult situations could be simplified if I were willing to relearn ways of handling them. This realization allowed me to lower the lofty expectations I had placed on myself. It really was all right if I didn't know how to handle all the new situations that motherhood had placed me in. So now if there is a particularly stressful situation in the family, I try to ask myself these questions:

- How much of the stress is being caused by my stubbornness in refusing to change my method of handling this situation—regardless of whether my solution is working or not? Have I based my solution on the unique personalities of my children and how my family work together, or on how I *think* the perfect family should work?
- If it's not my stubbornness blocking a solution, is it my inexperience?
- Am I willing to change my stance or my method and admit that maybe the way I've "always" done things doesn't work here?

Let's go back to my disastrous vacation. Because breaking a stressful situation into smaller parts helps to make it more manageable (more on that in the next section), that's where I started to work. I singled out each specific stresspoint to see how we could have handled things differently.

The length of our stay was a major stresspoint. Ever since I left home, over twenty years ago, my vacations to Florida were always spent with my mother and father. However, we had learned the hard way that no matter how much the grandparents long to see our little ones, a houseful of them with their noise and clutter gets overwhelming to people who are used to peace and privacy. We decided that our next trip would either have to be shorter, or we could try breaking up the time by spending a few days with other family members or even stay in a hotel for a few nights.

Another big stresspoint was my almost debilitating fatigue. One minute I was running around with the kids, sightseeing, and visiting family and friends; the next, I was doing laundry, dishes, and cleaning. Vacation is supposed to be a time for relaxing and getting away from the grind, but I discovered that moms can't do that completely. It usually takes some planning and compromising to make sure I get a break too.

For one thing, I needed to lower my expectations of the trip. My daydreams of sitting in the sun for hours with a good book (which is how I had "always" spent Florida vacations) had become totally unrealistic. I also needed to limit the number of activities I tried to take on. Sightseeing is not fun if you're exhausted.

David also had to relearn vacation expectations. Whereas it had previously been possible for him to take off for the day and fish or golf, he now had to accept some of the responsibility for seeing that I got some free time also. It would have been helpful to have had an agreement before the trip ever started as to what duties would be shared to make the vacation fun for everyone.

I learned to be creative and unconventional

in my relearning. When David was taking a business trip to the city where his parents live, he wanted to take the family with him. Having just recovered from our Florida trip, however, I asked him to think of some alternative to dragging us all down there. Our solution? He took two of the kids with him while I stayed home with the two youngest. People said to me, "But don't you want to get away too?" My unspoken answer was, Yes, I want to get away—from all the responsibility! With only two at home, I had a lot more freedom to come and go. I cleaned the house the day the others left, and it stayed clean for four entire days. The meals could be simpler and prepared on a looser schedule. The boys' afternoon nap time—the very nicest part of the day—left me with quiet time I hadn't known in years. In short, I had more of a vacation by staying home.

David also had a nice relearning experience. Previous to that trip, he would have claimed that he just couldn't handle the kids all on his own. Not only did he do a good job taking care of them, he had a wonderful time getting to know them better. In fact, he liked it so well that just a month later, he tried it again with a different combination of kids.

The biggest attitude I had to relearn was how I thought of my children. I hadn't realized until I started on the road to healing that they had lost their personhood to me. Then I was amazed at how little respect I had been showing them.

Yes, respect. Sometimes we fall into patterns

of sniping at our children until we come to the point where we are never cordial to them. We do not even afford them the common courtesy we would to a store clerk or gas-station attendant. My kids deserve better. They are people too.

Another attitude I had to relearn was thinking that if I was disorganized now, I would just always be disorganized. I suppose I felt if I was powerless to change my habit, people would just have to accept me for who I was, and I could avoid the struggle to change.

That worked just fine until the baby count kept rising. Then I found that if you are disorganized with four children to care for, you soon lose control of your house and family. I may have been able to get away with a lack of organization as a single or young-married, but now I do my family a disservice when I let things get out of hand. I would simply have to learn how to change. Once I had relearned my attitude on the possibility of change, the door was open for that change to occur. It has been a slow process, but at least I am now taking responsibility for it and not blaming it on some inborn, unchangeable character trait.

From the beginning of our walk with Christ, we have been relearning behavior and attitudes in all areas of our lives. He ultimately is the one who brings about change in us. Ask Him to show you where relearning can make you a more effective parent and a less-frustrated person. You'll be delighted at the burden of guilt you will shed when you can say, "I'm just a parent-in-progress. I don't know all the answers, but I'm willing to relearn!"

*Problem Solving in Parts.* One of the basics we learn in mathematics goes like this: "The whole is the sum of its parts." The "whole" usually gets all the attention, while the "parts" get relegated to bit-player status. Maybe in some areas of life this policy works, but in the areas of problem solving, we need to reverse the process.

Simply put, a problem broken down into its parts is easier to handle. In its entirety, the problem may prove so overwhelming it leaves us unable to act. Taken one at a time, however, the parts may prove quite manageable. In looking back, I can see where this method has helped me to deal with many of the problems I have faced.

The first example was in my depression itself. Just looking at the depression as one miserable whole, I had no idea where to begin "fixing" things. However, once I had broken it down into its various components—anger, resentment, and disappointment—I was able to see that there were solutions to the problems.

Breaking those emotions down into parts—as I had with my anger—made things clearer still. Defining the different kinds of anger I was experiencing helped me to find the different strategies I needed to deal with them.

I applied the part-strategy when I learned to organize my home. Looking at the laundry, the dishes, and the clutter as one whole unit facing me every single day, I came to the conclusion that I could never do it all. When I broke it down into parts—rooms, chores, days of the week—it quickly fit into a plan that didn't leave me feeling intimidated by my own house. My dwelling became mine again instead of some haunted horror house in which I felt trapped and threatened.

A third example of how this system works is in solving our vacation dilemma. Immediately after the vacation was over, we came to the decision that we would never, ever go anywhere with all six of us again. Because we were looking at the vacation as a whole, it made sense to say, "Family vacations don't work."

Luckily we took the time to ask ourselves, "Why don't they work?" That led us to look at the individual parts of the vacation, and from there it was a short step to finding solutions for the parts. As I discussed in a previous section, we realized that the length of our stay had been a problem. Solution: Shorten the trip or the time spent at individual homes. The fact that I felt like everyone else was getting a vacation while I was still running myself ragged was another problem. Solution: Ahead of time agree on a fair division of chores among the family members. Then limit side trips as much as possible. Fixing the parts, in this case, saved the "whole." We now know it is not necessary to do away with vacations until the children grow up.

This method may not help solve all problems, but it is worth analyzing whether the part-strategy would work in your situation. It will restore your sense of being in control when you find yourself looking at small parts of problems and methodically working them out one by one. The alternative—looking at a problem so large and overwhelming that you throw up your hands in defeat—quickly lowers your self-esteem.

# Chapter 8

## Identifying the Hot Spots

It's close to five o'clock in Anywhere, America. Mom stands by the hot stove, brushing the hair back from her sweaty brow, tensing at each shriek from the unhappy toddler in the next room. Because she has so little energy, she's cooking spaghetti—again. The new recipe she wanted to try sits unused on the countertop.

Her toddler knows the instant she starts preparing dinner. From that moment on, he stands by the gate that keeps him out of the kitchen and cries constantly until the meal is ready. She could let him into the kitchen and try to prepare dinner with him hanging onto her leg.

She calls the four-year-old to dinner and finds her asleep in front of the TV. One more day in which Mom has lost the battle of the nap. Now the little girl will be grumpy throughout dinner, but will get her second wind and be alert and lively until at least ten.

The scenario plays itself out in the old familiar way. She fixes everyone's plates; then before she can fix her own, everyone is clamoring for sec-

97

onds. She is up and down throughout the meal, eating her cold food on the run. Her stomach feels slightly upset as she tries to get the table cleared before the toddler gets into the salt or the butter. Then she bathes the children, gets them into their pajamas, and helps them clean up their toys. This always takes longer than she had planned. When at last she tries to snuggle peacefully beside them for the bedtime story, they want to talk, giggle, or bounce on the bed. It takes a while before they finally settle down for the night.

As she walks through the living room, her husband gets his "come hither" look as he makes room for her on the couch beside him. She fights back tears of frustration as she thinks of the dishes stacked in the kitchen and loads of laundry still sitting on the basement floor. As she does each evening, she will choose between two unsatisfying alternatives. If she chooses time with her husband, she will be up late with the housework or have to face it in the morning. If she chooses the housework, she will miss the quiet moment with him, and he will probably get his nose out of joint.

The evening I have described incorporates several of what I call the "Hot Spots." Hot Spots are those times of day, or regular events of the day, that we can count on to cause friction or stress whenever they occur. Every mother can identify herself somewhere at some time in the above story. Career mom or stay-at-home mom, mother of one, three, or six—we all sing our own version of the blues nearly every evening. I find that no matter how nice a day I might have had, once I have gone through this nightly ritual, I would tell anyone who asks that my day had been just awful.

One of my favorite book titles (and the book is great too!) is *I Need You Now, God, While the Grape Juice Is Running All Over the Floor*, by Dotsey Welliver. This woman knows Hot Spots! We instantly identify with her just from reading the title of her book. The surprising thing about Hot Spots is that they are universal. Mention one in a group of women, and you will get a roomful of groans in response.

Admittedly, this sounds repetitive, but you truly can relieve some of the stress simply by identifying those Hot Spots ahead of time. Give your Hot Spots a name and identify their characteristics. Don't just let them be some vague, intangible enemy waiting to pull a sneak attack on you. Name the Hot Spots and come up with ideas for handling them before the battle starts. And whatever wonderful ideas you come up with, be sure you remember to cover it all in a mantle of prayer.

I've chosen to list eight of my Hot Spots to help you get started on your own list, showing you ways I've learned to deal with them. Keep in mind two things: (1) Solutions to Hot Spots need constant review. Every time you think you have it aced, the kids have totally changed the game plan. (2) Just because you come up with some great ideas doesn't mean they will always work.

Sometimes you will blow it. Confess it and get on with your life. Whipping ourselves with guilt might feel good, but it is terribly unproductive.

*Hot Spot 1: Time for School*
The cause: The children don't want to get up, they don't like the clothes you picked out, they don't like the breakfast you fixed, they take forever putting on one pullover shirt, they wait until it's time to go before they tell you they can't find their shoes, and inevitably they run out the door just ahead of the bus. Have I left anything out?

The cure: It's ugly, I know, but you might just have to get up a half-hour earlier to get organized. Also, decide beforehand whether they get a vote in what they wear. Perhaps you could all choose their clothing the night before and lay it out, socks and underwear included. And don't forget the shoes! If they're with the rest of the clothes, they just might get put on before zero hour.

The truth is, I start out every morning calm and in control. I'm flexible on clothes. I'm flexible on breakfast. But when I go to help a child with his jacket and find they're still in their stocking feet, I flip. Dividing the morning into specific time periods has helped me. I wake the children one hour before they have to leave. (I don't have teenagers yet who need an entire hour to do their hair!) They then have thirty minutes to wake up and get dressed. During the first fifteen minutes, I pack lunches. (Some people find it relieves stress to pack the lunches the night before. I find that it gives me still one more thing to do in the evening, so I wait until the morning.) During the second fifteen minutes, I prepare breakfast.

At the end of the thirty minutes, I do a quick check to make sure the children are completely dressed. (For some reason, I always forget to check shoes!) Another helpful technique is to make sure they know there will be penalties for not completing their "assignment" in the time allotted. After losing after-dinner dessert a couple of times, my five-year-old suddenly learned how to dress a little more quickly.

Next they have fifteen minutes to eat, and the last fifteen minutes is devoted to combing hair, brushing teeth, and getting school supplies and jackets together. I'm still refining my method—and still need about twenty minutes to recuperate once they're gone—but the important part is that I'm working on it.

*Hot Spot 2: Now They're Home From School!*

The cause: The house has been very quiet. Peter is napping, and Danny plays quietly. I have been doing some writing or reading, and life feels good. Suddenly the doorbell starts ringing incessantly—they never believe I can hear it if it only rings once—and the peace is shattered. In the girls walk, tossing jackets, backpacks, and shoes in every direction. Every day I say, "Is that where they belong?" Every day they ignore me. Before I can repeat myself, they begin their clamoring—

"You have to sign this!" "Look at my paper!" "What can I eat?" "Can Kim come over?" "How come her friends can always come over?" "Where's my snack?" "You mean you let Danny play with my toys?" The five-year-old is crabby and takes it out on the three-year-old. The seven-year-old is calling people and inviting them over without asking me first. They head for the bathroom at the same time and have a shoving match at the door. In the midst of it all, Peter wakes up.

The cure: I'm still working on this one! It helps to start praying right before bus time. It doesn't take the Hot Spot away, but it does help you to gear up. I have realized that the abrupt change from peace to total chaos throws me. I take my break from my duties during the quiet time, and I am not prepared to be thrown back into the fray so quickly. Believe it or not, this Hot Spot contains one positive aspect; it does indeed get me back to work. If I go downstairs to do laundry or close myself in to clean the bathroom, it helps me to shut out the turmoil until I'm better able to handle it. By that time the kids will have moved off into their own activities, and the normal, everyday chaos will resume.

*Hot Spot 3: Preparing Dinner*

The cause: As described in the opening of this chapter, I'm trying to do a job that needs my hands and my mind. At the same time I have to keep track of a roaming toddler or suffer with him underfoot. Plus handle any disputes that come up. Plus keep the kindergartner from falling asleep. Plus deal with my resentment when David sits down with the newspaper, oblivious to the bedlam around him.

The cure: Use that honesty you learned in chapter 4. I used to stomp around the kitchen, banging pots and pans, just waiting for David to say, "What's wrong?" Then I could answer with an ominous, "Nothing." That kind of behavior doesn't solve the problem. Of course we'd like to think our husbands should be aware of the situation and, if they truly loved us, would offer their help. Logic would say, they're his kids, too, so why should we have to ask him to watch them? You will just have to swallow your pride. Say kindly, "I'm getting in a bind here. Could you watch the kids?" He'll probably say, "Sure, honey. Why didn't you say something?" Once he has said, "Sure," you can then say, "Go to Daddy," to every kid that passes through your kitchen with a problem.

*Hot Spot 4: The Dinner Table*

The cause: Mom is so busy she usually ends up with cold food. Dad can't stand the noise/bad manners/wasted food.

The cure: For Mom, the solution has become easy. Nearly every woman I have spoken to says that she now actually likes cold food.

For Dad, a little education might help him relax. It helped me immensely when I read that it is pointless to expect table manners from a child under six. Not that you shouldn't be teaching them—just don't expect your efforts to pay off immediately.

When a mother reads a statement like that, she remembers it forever. She can then relax, because she knows the behavior is not caused by a glaring omission on her part. Dad will have to be reminded of this developmental principle at least once a week. And if he's like my husband, every time he hears it, he will say, "Really?" as though it's totally new to him.

Use your honesty tack here too. Tell hubby that you need his help serving the kids so that you will have time to enjoy your meal. So many of us wait until we're at the table and then either glare at our husbands the entire time we're working or snap something like, "Can't you help?" If you've talked it through, you just need to gently remind him if he forgets. It really does make life more pleasant.

One can learn a lot of practical tactics that parents use to keep dinnertime mayhem to a minimum. Two good places to learn these tips are by asking your own friends or by checking the reader-contribution sections of parenting magazines.

*Hot Spot 5: Bath and Bed*

The cause: Getting four kids bathed in one evening can be a major undertaking. And coping with reluctant children at bedtime is especially stressful, because by that time you have allowed yourself to believe that peace and quiet are just around the corner.

The cure: The best stress-reliever of all came when my husband decided he would start doing the evening dishes. Now I don't feel like the work before me will take all night. He does the kitchen; I do the kids. Then we can enjoy the rest of the evening together.

As for the bedtime blues, I don't know what the experts would think of my solution. The girls simply would not go to sleep in the same room, preferring to talk and giggle until all hours. Even spanking did nothing to quiet them, and it just upset us to have to do it. Now I put one of them to sleep in my bed and carry her to her own when she's asleep. Something in my gut tells me I must be copping out, but the truth is, I don't care. Bedtimes are much more peaceful now, and the girls are getting the sleep they need.

### Hot Spot 6: Church Time

The cause: I think every mother I ever talked to cites attending church services as a major cause of tension. Getting everyone ready and out the door on time leaves nerves so frayed that you wonder why you're even going to church. Another Hot Spot for us occurs at the fellowship time after the service. So many children are running around that it becomes difficult to keep track of your own. One day Peter walked out with another family. Luckily, they returned him. Another day I found him outside in the parking lot playing in the rain.

Because this is one of the few times I have to

chat with some of my church friends, I feel resentful when I have to interrupt conversations to look for a missing child.

The cure: We have discussed the possibility of going right home after church, but decided the fellowship is important. Since David usually stresses out first, I have to remember that my needing to talk to "one last person" could be the straw that breaks David's back. We have a signal—very unsophisticated and to the point. David says the words "breaking point," and I know it's time to help him gather up kids.

We are still working on how to get out of the house and to the church without the customary battles. Surely someone has found a way to do it without all the tension!

*Hot Spot 7: Traveling*

The cause: Whatever way you are traveling, children have special needs and require special handling. They do not settle down just because the businessman on the airplane has work to do. They do not willingly forego dinner just because Dad wants to drive straight through. And they hate sleeping on the seats in the train.

The cure: I will direct you to the many books written on this subject for truly expert help. But one thing you must do is plan ahead. Anticipate the problems that could arise and ahead of time plan ways to deal with them. When your husband is barreling down the highway at freeway speed is not the time to argue about whether you're stopping for dinner. Plan your agenda, but always remain flexible.

### Hot Spot 8: Sex

The cause: Do I need to say it? Fatigue has robbed you of the desire. The fear of interruption has inhibited you. And the need to plan ahead has spoiled the wonderful spontaneity.

The cure: Even more books have been written on this subject. I will just mention a couple of things. The wife has to guard against making her husband feel rejected or less important to her than the children. While she may feel a desire for sexual intimacy only three or four times a month, she should make an effort to respond to him more often. The husband should learn not to take it personally when his wife's passion is at a low ebb. It is normal with all the demands being placed on her life right now, and it will improve with time. Try to be intimate in ways that do not have to end in sex.

A terrible cycle begins when the wife feels pressured, the husband feels neglected, and they end up losing their ability to be intimate on any level. Remember to keep communication open, and don't let hurt feelings fester.

My list of Hot Spots should help you get started compiling your own list—or thinking of your own ways to handle the ones I've mentioned. Hot Spots don't need to sabotage your sanctification! I know they seem like booby traps on the path of life, but we can learn to defuse Hot Spots if we're willing to put forth the effort.

# Chapter 9

## Consider It All Joy

Peter was eighteen months old. Which means he could be classified as one of the seven great terrors of the world. He worked hard at living up to the name. Today he was bored with his blocks and baby toys. He wanted something more interesting. So when he noticed that someone had forgotten to close Mom's bedroom door, he quickly took advantage of the moment.

There were lots of fun things to do in this room, and Peter stopped only a moment to make his choice among them. There was Mom's dresser, which by standing on tiptoe, he could just reach. She had baskets full of pretty things that his chubby little fingers could close around. There was also the box of videotapes under her dresser. If all else failed, there was the closet, where a boy could sit for ages and find things to fool around with.

But wait, what was this? Some kind of large box lay in the middle of the floor, with clothes and shoes neatly tucked into it. He was too young to know it was a suitcase, but he wasn't too young to figure out ways to enjoy it.

He walked around it once, surveying it closely, taking stock of its possibilities. Very carefully Peter lifted one foot and placed it over the side, setting it down again in the middle of the box. The clothes had a nice squooshy feeling. Trying to balance himself, he lifted his other foot and pulled it into the box. Losing his balance, he plopped down into the fluffy pillow of clothes. He bounced up and down a couple of times before inspecting the shoes that were tucked into the sides and corners.

When it got a little boring, he heaved his little body out of the box. There must be something else you could do with a box like this, he seemed to be thinking. Aha! Look at the wonderful kaleidoscope of colors and textures it made when you threw everything up in the air at once.

It was then that Mom came into the room. He grinned broadly at her, not seeming to notice the look of horror on her face. "Petey!" she shrieked, startling him. "My suitcase!" He recovered quickly, laughed at her, and turned to run into the far corner of the room. He stood there and watched her as she folded the things and placed them back in the box, all the while muttering to herself. Every once in a while she would look up and glare at him. Every time she did, he smiled all the more.

Finally, when she had the suitcase repacked, her mood seemed to lighten, and she smiled at him. "You're looking for big trouble, aren't you?" she said, shaking a finger at him. "I think I'll just work in here where I can keep an eye on you." She began to make the bed.

Since she didn't seem to be noticing him anymore, he wandered out of the corner. He wondered if he could get her attention by playing with the pretty clothes again. He toddled over to the box and began to pitch clothes out of it. Peter was only halfway through this time when she grabbed him. "Leave my suitcase alone!" She commanded, as she picked him up and set him back in the corner.

While she was busy repacking, his gaze slowly left her and moved to the bed she had just made. He loved the smooth, soft look of the sheets when they were spread out like that, with that pretty flowered bedspread folded on top of them. He climbed silently up onto the bed. She still wasn't noticing him. He moved into the middle of the bed, where he could see himself in the large mirror. Peter smiled at the reflection of the baby who, much to his delight, smiled back at him. He began to bounce softly on the bed, and when the baby in the mirror began to bounce with him, he bounced even harder. Soon he began to run around in a little circle, and in his glee he reached down and scooped up an armful of sheets.

Suddenly Mom was grabbing him again, dragging him off the bed, and plunking him on the floor. This was getting monotonous. He couldn't understand why she was doing all that muttering, this time at the sheets she was smoothing over. Why didn't big people smile when they were doing something fun like smoothing sheets?

Oh, well, he hadn't played with anything on the dresser yet. He headed toward it since she was busily straightening the bed and had obviously forgotten him. First he made a stop at the videotapes and pulled a few of them out, but that game lost its appeal quickly. He could never get any of the tapes out of their boxes, and that was the only time it was really any fun.

Finally he looked up on the dresser. There he found a little bottle of pink stuff that looked fun to play with, so he quietly pulled it down. Mom looked up and saw him, but in her frazzled state she decided, "I guess you can play with that; the lid is on tight," and went on with her work. The letters on the bottle said "Collagen Hand and Body Lotion—1 ounce," but he wasn't interested in that. The little black cap on the top of the bottle had captured his attention. He had by this time learned that caps are what keep the goodies inside a bottle, so he began to worry with it. At first it wouldn't budge, but eventually he felt it begin to turn ever so slightly. A little more playing around, and he had it off. Quickly, because he knew that Mom always took bottles away from him if the caps were off, he placed the bottle to his lips. The pink stuff was smooth and rather pleasant tasting, so he tilted the bottle and let it run down onto his tongue.

Another shriek from Mom. "What are you doing?" She grabbed him. He watched her examine the bottle, holding it up to the light to see if there was anything in it. When she couldn't tell anything from that, she suddenly stuck her nose in his mouth. "Oh, you did drink it," she cried. "Why did you do that?"

He laughed at her again and reached out to tweak her nose. He liked this new game.

Ever have a day like that? This particular incident occurred while I was trying to get ready for a special trip. David and I were going away for three days to celebrate our tenth anniversary. It was our first trip alone since we had children, and I was really looking forward to it. David was approaching it with visions of romance in his head, but I had visions of peace and quiet.

The hand lotion episode was only the first of many obstacles that threatened to rob us of our dreams. The hotel we had chosen was undergoing renovations; consequently, their restaurant was closed, and there was clutter everywhere. Our room, much smaller than we had expected, had a view of a back-door service entrance. It stormed so hard the first night we were there that we couldn't go out as we had planned, and then the entree room service sent was so salty we could barely eat it.

There was a time when a combination of all those little trials would have totally destroyed the weekend for me. I had become so negative in my parenting that I looked at each new disruption as further proof that I was doomed to a life of unhappiness. I simply could not cope with situations that got out of control or didn't go completely as planned.

We all know the person who is constantly moaning, "Why me? Why do these things always happen to me?" Every time the car breaks down or the dishwasher springs a leak or the garbage man forgets the trash, this person's entire day is ruined and his or her moaning ruins everyone else's day.

That used to describe my mothering. When Peter spilled his grape juice down the front of my dress at the church, I had to dash to the bathroom to hide my tears. There I berated myself in the mirror with, "That's what you get for thinking you can handle four kids in public. You shouldn't bother trying to go out at all." I was so caught up in the drama of "Poor-Me" that I couldn't simply grab a towel and say, "Oh well; with kids around, spills will happen."

I was able to see that God was working in me when I began to both handle these unexpected disruptions and also learn from them. James 1:2 tells us to "consider it all joy . . . when you encounter various trials; knowing that the testing of your faith produces endurance. And let endurance have its perfect result, that you may be perfect and complete, lacking in nothing" (NASB).

When I was always angry at my children, the little upsets just increased my anger and became yet one more occasion for yelling or some other immature reaction. I did not look at the interruptions as an opportunity for character development, but rather as proof that life was playing a cruel joke on me. But James says that God wants us to have joy; even though life may be full of trials, they can be used to make us into stronger people. When we are in the middle of a pity party, we miss the chance to grow through the challenges our children present us. Is it any wonder such parents lead joyless lives?

It's not fun to find yourself in the middle of a carefully planned event that suddenly comes apart at the seams. But how we react makes a big difference in our attitude toward those little gifts from God who are usually the reason things are out of control.

For example, our family was asked to light the candle at the first advent service this year. We offered to leave one or both of the boys in the nursery, but the program coordinator assured us the entire family was to participate. So we decided that I would light the candle and then try to keep the children quiet while David did the reading. When I lighted the candle, little Peter looked on in awe, while the other three stood quietly beside their dad. I actually let the thought slip through my mind, "This is going well."

David stepped behind the large pulpit and began to read, and I gathered my brood around me to listen. Suddenly baby Peter was struggling to be put down, the five- and three-year-olds were heading in opposite directions, and Elizabeth had taken it upon herself to go after the three-year-old and drag him back. I'm sure the reading took two minutes at most, but it felt more like hours. When I saw Danny head for the baptismal font, I stuffed the baby into the pulpit at David's feet, at which point David went on automatic pilot and was barely conscious of what he was reading. I then retrieved Danny and stuffed him in beside his brother. During the rest of the reading I used my hands to control the girls and my foot to push escaping boys back into their pen.

I'm going to be honest with you. I wish my kids were angelic types, or at least obedient types, who stand where you put them and won't move until given the signal. But they aren't. There was a time when I would have been filled with anger at having been subjected to public agony like that. Instead, I now consider it all joy—for two reasons.

First, I have learned to rejoice in the uniqueness of my family. My children are bubbly, curious, independent kids. And that is what I want them to be. So I refuse to discipline them for their exuberance simply because I am worried what other people think of them or my mothering ability. That does not mean they got off scotfree for their behavior in front of the church. What it does mean is that I have accepted my children and myself for who we are, and I love us.

The second reason I rejoice is that I can see God working patience and endurance into my character through trials like these. I didn't run to the restroom to cry this time. I shrugged my shoulders and laughed. And a lot of people laughed with me.

Scripture says the joy of the Lord is my strength (see Nehemiah 8:10). If I am not feeling joy in my family, it can usually be traced to feelings of weakness and defeat. Those feelings mean that I have not plugged in to my divine power supply. When I have His joy, I am strong. When I am strong, I have His joy. It is a never-ending circle.

Next to salvation, our children are the greatest gift we receive. Their mere existence is cause for celebration. The cute and loving things they do fill us with happiness. But there's a whole lot of stuff in between the good times. It does us no good to grit our teeth through the ordinary and the bad times, thinking our strength comes from the good. If James is right, the real work is done during the bad times. We have to learn to consider it *all* joy—the good and the bad.

If the promise of endurance doesn't sound like a great bonus to you, consider the result of that endurance. We will eventually become perfect and complete, lacking in nothing (see James 1:2-4; 5:11). Parents who have set their sights on the goals of completeness and perfection—rather than being content to stagnate in anger, resentment, and disappointment—have a wonderful gift to give their children.

# Epilogue

"But, Lord, I'm not ready to do that yet."

I was probably trying to convince myself as much as I was trying to convince God. I had always been an active person, willing to take on new challenges even when they scared me. But with my fourth baby and the ensuing depression, I had slowly slipped out of circulation. Then when the healing process had started, it had taken all my energy just to get my life and home back in order. I had no energy to spare, so I focused almost exclusively on myself and my family.

Dropping all extras had been the right thing to do. Like a person who has had major surgery (which it sometimes felt God was performing on me), I had needed time to rest and let healing take place.

As I learned how to be a better person and a better mom, I came to the place where I was coping with the challenges of life again. I also have to admit, I was enjoying the cocoon that I had built around myself. Once I had learned how to say No to people, I got so good at it that I could say it without thinking.

Now God seemed to be drawing me back into the world of my church and community again. Within a three-week period, every book I read and every sermon that I heard seemed to have something to say about getting into service for God. I kept hearing about the danger of becoming too self-absorbed, forgetting about people who need to know about the God who has changed our lives.

In one book, which I had intended to read for entertainment value, the author made the statement that a childless woman can be more fruitful than one who is absorbed with her family. It was the last straw. "OK, OK, Lord," I thought. "I think I'm getting the message."

In some ways, getting back into wider involvement is a scary idea. It means leaving my safe little nest and going into unknown territory. It means putting a strain on my time and emotions again.

On the other hand, not so very long ago I felt trapped by my home and family. Just the fact that I now thought of it as my "safe little nest" showed me how far I had come. I had to tell myself that if God was urging me out of that nest, it could mean only one thing: I had been making progress. If He was asking me to put my time and emotions at risk, it could mean only one thing: He wouldn't ask me to do something He hadn't prepared me for. He wouldn't ask more of me than I was capable of performing.

I don't intend to dive in headfirst. My family is

still young, and they don't need a mom who is driving herself back to the brink of fatigue and emotional wipeout. I can start getting my feet wet, however. God has already shown me where to get started, and I'm very excited about it.

Besides having the joy of mothering restored to me as a result of the difficult time I went through, I was also reminded of what a wonderful God I serve. Knowing that the sovereign God of the universe has chosen to dwell in this humble homemaker, and—better yet—to take an active part in my life, is almost more than I can comprehend. I am eager for the next chapter.

# Recommended Reading

Alcorn, Randy and Nanci. *Women Under Stress: Preserving Your Sanity.* Multnomah Press, 1986.

Arndt, Elise. *A Mother's Touch.* Victor Books, 1983.

Barnes, Emilie. *The Creative Home Organizer.* Harvest House Publishers, 1988.

Barnes, Marilyn Gwaltney. *Love (and Baby Powder) Covers All.* Campus Crusade, 1985.

Dobson, Dr. James. *Dare to Discipline.* Tyndale House Publishers, 1973.

Fleming, Jean. *A Mother's Heart.* Navpress, 1982.

Henrichsen, Walter A. *How to Disciple Your Children.* Victor Books, 1981.

Howard, J. Grant. *Balancing Life's Demands: A*

*New Perspective on Priorities.* Multnomah Press, 1983.

LaHaye, Tim. *Spirit-Controlled Temperament.* Tyndale House Publishers, 1966.

Lewis, Deborah Shaw. *Motherhood Stress.* Word Books, 1989.

Lutzer, Erwin. *Managing Your Emotions.* Victor Books, 1983.

Welliver, Dotsey. *I Need You Now, God, While the Grape Juice Is Running All Over the Floor.* Light and Life Press, 1975.

# Good health never tasted so good!

*Life's Simple Pleasures* redefines good eating and good times by providing complete seasonal menus (more than 140 mouthwatering, low-cholesterol, vegetarian recipes) that are easy to prepare and perfect for entertaining.

Spectacular color photographs stimulate the imagination of the creative host or hostess, returning joy to the kitchen and excitement to the dining table.

An excellent gift idea, *Life's Simple Pleasures* is more than a cookbook. It's a celebration of the good life.

**US$24.95/Cdn$31.20.** Hardcover, 160 pages.

Please photocopy and complete the form below.